ENVIRONMENT IMPACT ASSESSMENT FOR WETLAND PROTECTION

V.S. Kulkarni **S.N. Kaul**

National Environmental Engineering
Research Institute, Nehru Marg,
NAGPUR - 440 020

R.K. Trivedy

Reader & In-charge
Pollution Studies Deptt.
Y.C. College of Science, KARAD-415 110

SCIENTIFIC
PUBLISHERS

Published by:

Scientific Publishers
5A, New Pali Road, P.O. Box 91
Jodhpur 342 001, India
E-mail: info@scientificpub.com
Website: www.scientificpubonlione.com

Print : 2025

ISBN: 978-81-7233-293-8

Lasrtypeset : Rajesh Ojha
Printed in India

PREFACE

Wetlands are transitional areas between aquatic and terrestrial ecosystems where the water table is usually at or near the surface, or the land is covered by shallow water. Wetlands are among the most productive life support systems in the world and are of immense socio-economic and ecological importance to mankind. In India wetlands are distributed in different geographical regions.

Wetlands play critical role in the improvement of water quality through the arrest of pollutants (organic & inorganic) from direct release to the natural water bodies and by removal of sediments, production of oxygen, recycling of nutrients, and treatment of wastewater by removing nitrogen, phosphorus, bacteria and viruses. The wetlands act as habitat for fish & shellfish, and for birds, mammals, reptiles & amphibians, many of which are of economic value in terms of subsistence and commercial fishing, hunting and trapping. Non-consumptive uses of the wetlands, viz. bird watching, recreation, aesthetics, educational activities, and scientific research are also well recognized.

Population pressures in the past few decades led to rapid utilization of natural resources for land based development. In this process wetlands were treated with contempt. Ignoring their importance, wetlands were considered obstacles in the path of progress and reservoirs of diseases. Wetlands were hence drained, filled and reclaimed for more economic gains. The rivers were dammed, regulated and channellized leading to modification or elimination of floodplains. This led to a considerable alteration of wetland habitats and the composition of associated flora and fauna. A select list of activities that affected wetlands is presented in Table - 1.

In the recent past importance of wetlands has been realized by the policy makers worldover and efforts are being made to protect the wetlands from further deterioration and loss.

Environmental Impact Assessment (EIA) is potentially one of

the most valuable, inter-disciplinary and objective decision-making tools with respect to alternate routes for development, process technologies and project sites. It is an anticipatory mechanism which establishes quantitative values for parameters indicating the quality of the environment and natural systems before, during and after the proposed developmental activity, thus allowing measures ensuring environmental compatibility and economic efficacy. EIA is designed to present a clear and concise picture of all benefits and costs associated with alternative courses of action, and thus provides a mechanism for merging concerns for ecology and economics in the process of decision-making.

In many cases developmental activities adversely affect wetland benefits which are of value to communities and natural processes. EIA can provide very useful information on how wetlands will be affected by the proposed developmental activities to ensure effective management of wetlands. EIA can help planners make rational decisions about resource allocation and ensure that the wetland benefits required for sustainable development are maintained.

The objective of this manual is to assist project proponents, conservation activists and decision makers to identify the wetland benefits present at a particular site as also benefits which are likely to be adversely affected by a particular project activity. This would enable assessing the extent and cost of the management plan required to mitigate these impacts.

With the backdrop of international conventions for wetland protection and initiatives of the Ministry of Environment and Forests, Government of India, manual delineates step by step procedure for EIA of developmental activities affecting wetland benefits. Worksheets that could enable preparation of case studies are included in the manual. Four casestudies prepared by the institutions that participated in the March 1995 workshop organized by the British Council, at Calcutta, have been included in the manual.

28th August, 2000

V.S. Kulkarni
S.N. Kaul
R.K. Trivedy

INTRODUCTION

CONCEPT OF EIA

The sociocultural roots of the present environmental crisis lie in the paradigms of scientific materialism and economic determinism which fail to recognize the physical limits imposed by ecological systems on economic activity. The economies must expand within ecosystems which have limited regenerative capacities. Contrary to the neoclassical theory of continuous material growth, economic activities directly undermine the potential for development through over-exploitation of natural resources, and indirectly compromise future production through the discharge of residuals. The entrenchment with quantitative growth as a major instrument of social policy in thus quite paradoxical (Khanna, 1989).

The emergence of the concept of sustainable development in recent years has brought in the general realization that societal perceptions must shift towards ecological determinism so as to achieve growth within the limits of ecosystem carrying capacity. The carrying capacity based planning process, innovative technologies for enhanced material and energy effectively of production and consumption, structural economic change towards less resource-intensive sectors, and preventive environmental management through increasingly interventionist policies are some of the strategies for reconciling developmental goals with ecological capabilities (Khanna and Kulkarni, 1992).

Environmental impact assessment is potentially one of the most valuable, inter-disciplinary, and objective decision making tools with respect to alternate routes for development, process technologies and project sites. It is an ideal anticipatory mechanism allowing measurtes that ensure environmental compatibility in our quest for socio-economic development.

There is no universally accepted definition of EIA. Some commonly used definitions are :

- EIA consists in establishing quantitative values for selected parameters which indicate the quality of the environment before, during, and after the action (Heer & Hagerty, 1977).
- EIA is an assessment of all relevant environmental and resulting social effects which would result from a project (Battelle, 1978).
- EIA is an activity designed to identify and predict the impact on the biogeophysical environment and on Man's health and well being of legislative proposals, policies, programmes, projects and operational procedures, and to interpret and communicate information about impacts (Munn, 1979).
- EIA is a process to identify, predict and to descrive in appropriate terms the pros and cons (benefits and penalties) of a proposed development. To be useful, the assessment needs to be communicated in terms understandable by the community and decision-makers and the pros and cons should be identified on the basis of criteria relevant to the countries affected (UNEP, 1980).
- EIA is the systematic examination of environmental consequences of projects, policies, plans and programmes. Its main aim is to provide decision-makers with an account of implications of alternative courses of action before a decision is made (Clark, 1984).
- EIA is a formal study process used to predict the environmental consequences of the proposed developmental project, find ways to reduce unacceptable impacts, and shape the project so that it suits the local environment, and present these predictions and options to decision-makers (UNEP, 1988).

The definition proposed by Hear and Hagerty forms the basis of present research. EIA is a process that has the objective of providing decision makers with an indication of the likely consequences of their actions. This is achieved through impact identification, prediction, evaluation and mitigation stages which endeavour to answer the questions : What will happen as a result of the project?, what will be the extent of the changes?, do the changes matter?, and what can be done about them? (UNEP, 1988).

Over the years, it has become increasingly clear that the

environmental clearance of the project proposals by the competent authority is not the sole decision point in EIA. Decision making starts much earlier, may be at the stage of selection of raw materials and production process, and extends to feedback mechanisms in the form of environmental monitoring during the operation phase. In the past, attention has tended to focus on envrionmental clearance, and the importance of a well-integrated appraisal in the refinement of project proposals has largely been under-valued (Wathern, 1988).

However, EIA is no longer seen as an add-on process. The greatest contribution of EIA to environmental management is in reducing adverse impacts by devising measures, beyond those warranted by emission standards and environmental management regulations, through the application of tools such as impact identification and use of mathematical models for impact prediction before the project proposal is submitted for environmental appraisal. It is now generally accepted throughout the world that the benefits of project level EIA considerably outweigh its costs (Wathern, 1988; Biswas and Agarwala, 1992; Wood, 1994). In recent years, the outcome of EIA studies ranges from simple impact statements to changes in project sites, manufacturing processes, raw materials, engineering designs, introduction of additional pollution control measures, landscaping, manpower training programmes, compensation for restoration of damaged resources, and off-site programs to enhance quality of life of the community likely to be affected due to proposed developmental activity.

HIERARCHY IN EIA

The EIA studies for industrial projects could be categorized as site selection studies, rapid/comprehensive/regional EIAs, and carrying capacity studies.

Site selection studies involve evaluation of the alternative sites with respect to environmental and project attributes such as proximity to raw materials, infrastructural facilities, markets etc. The study aims at ranking of site alternatives for objective decision making.

Rapid EIA differs from Comprehensive EIA with respect to time frame for baseline data collection. Rapid EIA refers to assessment based on one season (3 months) monitoring whereas Comprehensive EIA relates to assessment based on three seasons (9 months) monitoring for baseline data. Rapid EIA facilities decision-making in those situations where a fair amount of knowledge exists about the proposed site or the impacts of the proposed development. Rapid EIA also helps in identifying significant issues for comprehensive EIA.

Regional EIA relates to development in/of a region based on three season data collection and addresses itself to the analysis of assimilative capacity of air, water and land components of environment. The scope of carrying capacity study is extended to the analysis of supportive capacity in the region with respect to resource availability\utilization, supply/demand, infrastructure/congestion, and assimilative capacity/residuals.

MAJOR ISSUES IN EIA

EIA has been regarded as both science and art, reflecting the concern related to technical aspects of appraisal ad the effects of EIA upon the decision making process (Kennedy, 1984). Further, decisions are often shaped rather than made or taken. Everyone involved in policy formulation, planning and impact assessment studies as well as in public hearings, reviews, legislative/media debates is in fact playing a part in shaping decisions (Munn, 1979). The decision of an effective EIA methodology can be envisaged as the search for mechanisms to deal with issues generated by the need to juxtapose the planning and environmental clearance of project proposals. Some issues deal with technical matters such as impact identification and prediction while others relate to the management of information. The major issues in EIA process are :

* Identification of projects requiring EIA
* Identification of impacts to be assessed
* Assessment of impacts'
* Completion of an appraisal
* Enabling the objectivity in appraisal

The structure of an EIA process is dictated primarily by the need to accommmodate these issues as illustrated in Figure 1 (Wathern, 1988).

From the technical point of view, EIA can be considered as a data management process. It has three components. First, the appropriate information necessary for a particular decision to be taken must be identification and, possibly, collected. Secondly, changes in environmental parameters resulting from the implementation of the project must be determined and compared with the situation likely to accrue without the project. Finally, actual change must be recorded and analysed.

The most important problem in EIA is the availability of appropriate EIA methodology. More than fifty impact assessment

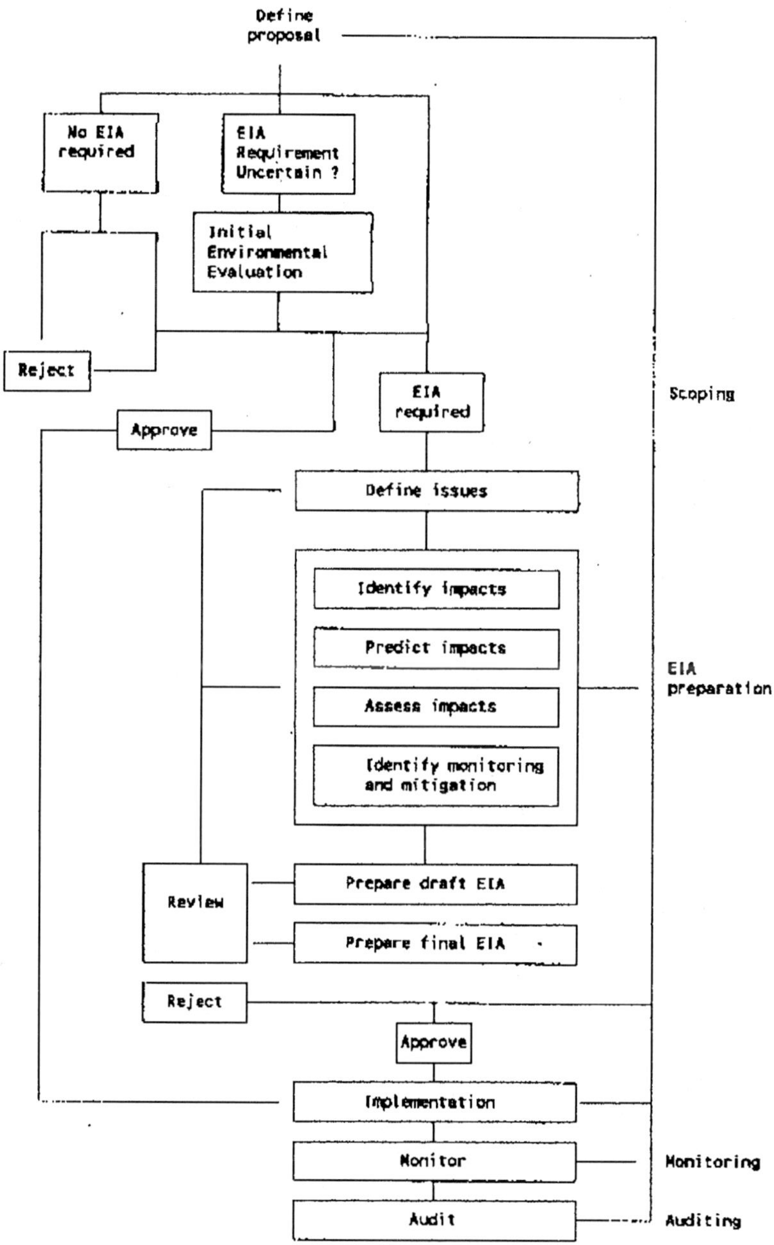

Fig. 1. Flow Diagram Showing the Main Components of an EIA system

methodologies have been developed so far but no universal methodology is yet available for internalising environmental concerns in planning process.

Available methodologies for EIA; which include checklists, matrics and networks; perform the task of identification of potential impacts. Mathematical modelling helps in prediction of impacts. Batelle Environmental Evaluation system and UNEP Test Model achieve the evaluation step: None of the methodologies, available singly, satisfactorily achieve the necessary three steps. Further, if essential to evolve a methodology that would lend itself to the integration of environmental concerns in the process of socio-economic development.

SCOPE FOR USE OF COMPUTERS IN EIA

Experience over the years has shown that EIAs are always conducted under severe limitations of time, manpower, financial resources, and data (Khanna, 1989).

In the past, the major role of computers in EIA was limited to the prediction step. However, computers can be used in all the stages of EIA, viz. impact identification, prediction, evaluation and mitigation.

The most logical way of identifying impacts associated with the project is through establishing cause-condition-effect networks. The complex nature of industrial processes warrant thorough knowledge of the transformation processes as also environmental risks associated with various activities in pinpointing the impacts of developmental projects and optimizing the data requirements of EIA.

Mathematical models for prediction of air, water and noise environment are available in literature. However, the software packages incorporating these models have failed to keep pace with the modifications on the mathematical sciences. Further, these packages were not developed for EIA as such, are not user- friendly, and the out-come of the models need interpretation by experts. Most of the packages were developed in 1970s using FORTRAN, and the subsequent modifications have also relied on FORTRAN.

Scaling-weighting methods for impact evaluation facilities aggregation of impacts to yield a score representing the net environmental impact of a project alternative. However, these methods warrant selection of parameters relevant to the project under consideration from a comprehensive list of parameters, computation of environmental quality for all selected parameters using value function curves, and assigning weights (parameter importance units) to the selected parameters through ranked pairwise comparison. Computational and data requirements of these methods have largely kept them at bay practioners of EIAs.

While the methodology for design of green-belt for attenuation of fugitive air emissions is very well documented, it is not commonly used due to complex mathematics involved in optimizing the width of green-belts. Since early 1980s, with the advent of personal computers (PC-XT to Pentium, monochrome to SVGA monitors) on one hand and availability of computer languages such as BASIC, Pascal and C which enable software development in interpretation mode and use of colours for screen display on other, computers have opened a wide vista to overcome the problems faced by the practioners of EIAs.

SCOPE OF CURRENT RESEARCH

The proposed research addresses itself to the development of a tool to provide scientific inputs to the process of EIA of industrial projects as a decision making tool through the development and computerization of methods for impact identification, prediction, evaluation and mitigation. The work has been organized into four parts :

* Literature review to screen available methodologies and software packages
* Development of methodology for EIA, and computer software package EIA-AID on Personal Computer platform
* Development of sensitivity analysis to assess uncertainty in impact prediction and evaluation, and computerization of the same
* Validation of EIA-AID through a case study

The literature review traces the evolution of EIA worldwide and in India, analyses documented literature on site selection criteria, screening of projects for EIA, EIA methodologies, impact quantification techniques, and the scope for enlarged role of project level EIA.

Incorporating the best features of various EIA methodologies and prediction models a user-friendly PC based software package, acronymed EIA-AID, has been developed in Quick Basic 4.5 in this research to assist EIA teams. Salient features of EIA-AID are :

* The screening module enables selection of projects for rapid/comprehensive EIA based on the project threshold database developing during this research and inbuilt in the programme. The

module also enable preliminary screening of site options based on siting guidelines developed in this research.

* The site selection module enables ranking of project site alternative based on the considerations of regional assimilative capacity, supportive capacity, and project attributes. The methodology developed in this research, and incorporated in the module, uses the concept of scaling-weighing of impacts for ranking of site alternatives. The user has the options to either use in-built scaling functions and weights or define project specific ones in an interactive mode. Weights are assigned through an interactive ranged pairwise comparision technique. The structural mode of programme also facilities scaling function database modification using the text-editor.

* The impact identification module incorporates the best features of questionnaire and descriptive checklists as also the concept of cause-condition-effect networks. The module enables identification of primary, secondary, and tertiary impacts trigerred by the project activities. The data requirements, sources of data, and tools for data analysis are also included. Adequate quidence is provided to the user on standard practices of environmental monitoring.

* The prediction modules for air, noise and water quality enable generation of scenarios of environmental quality after the project implementation.

* The air quality prediction module provides options to select screening model for desing of monitoring networks, short-term predictions (1 hr, 8 hr and 24 hr average), sequential modelling, and long-term impact predictions based on stability rose data. The module incorporates state of the art versions of Gaussian Plume Model, wind extrapolation formulae, plume rise formulae, dispersion coefficients (Urban/rural areas), and terrain variations (flat/complex/valley). These models handle upto 40 sources at a time provide online guidance for input data, and generate output that does not warrant expert-interpretation. Salient features of the module lies in enabling the user to select different spatical resoultion in the impact zone (distance between a grid of 480 receptors located in 16 wind directions).

* The noise prediction module enables assessment of impact of stationary noise sources on a grid of 900 receptors defined in cartesian co-ordinate system. In addition, the user can specify the location of sensitive receptors (Maximum 10 nos.). The module takes into account attenuation due to air absorbtion, physical barriers (defined by the user in two dimensions), and vegetation.

The module outputs the impact of individual as also combined effect of noise sources. Both equivalent and day-night noise levels are computed. The module also computes the width of green- belt to attenuate noise levels.

* The water quality prediction module incorporates the self-calibrating model developed in the present research, and enables assessment of impact of carbonaceous and nitrogenous BOD on dissolved oxygen, impact of non-conservative pollutants with first order decay coefficients, and conservative pollutants for rivers/streams. The most significant features of the module lie in availability of deoxygeneration and reaeration coefficients reported in literature, computation of the coefficients based on selection of appropriate in built formulae, and calibrates coefficients based on field data. In addition, it provides choice to over-ride all these computations to select coefficients based on user's judgment with project scenario where these coefficients may change significantly based on site-specific conditions and waste characteristics.
* The impact evaluation module incorporates a methodology developed in the present research by extending the concepts of Leopold matrix and Battele Environmental Evaluation System (BEES). The impact of project is quantified in terms of changes in ecological, pollution, aesthetics, and socio-economic indices. These indices are then converted in numerical scores for assessing the overall impact.
* The sensitivity analysis module enables the user to assess the subjectivity in assigning weights in impact evaluation to delineate maximum/minimum weights that could be assigned to an individual environmental category/component/parameter.
* The green-belt module enables optimization of the width of green-belt for abatement of fugitive emissions with different tree species and atmospheric stabilities.

In order to assess the uncertainty in impact prediction, sensitivity analysis have been carried out for :

* Design of air quality monitoring networking for multiple point sources
* Changes in maximum ground level concentrations of air pollutants due to :
  - changes in mixing height variations
  - changes in dispersion coefficients as a function of terrain variations

- changes in wind extrapolation factors as a function of terrain variations
- sequential analysis (averaging period 24 hours in calender day Vs any 24 hours slot in study period)

* Impact zone for industrial noise sources
* Changes in dissolved oxygen deficit in receiving body of water due to :
  - variations in longitudinal dispersion
  - variationns in deoxygenation coefficient
  - variations in reaeration coefficient

The software EIA-AID, developed in the present research, has been validated through a real-life case study.

REFERENCES

Biswas, A.K., and Agarwala, S.B.C., 1992. Environmental Impact Assessment for Developing Countries, Butterworth-Heinemann, Oxford

Battele Institute, 1978. The Selection of projects for EIA, Commission of the Europian Communities Environment and Consumer Protection Service, Brussels

Clark, B.D., 1984. Environmental Impact Assessment : Scope and objectives in Perspective in Environmental Impact Assessment, D. Reidel Publishing Company, Holland

Heer, J.E. and Hagerty, D.J. 1977. Envrionmental Assessment and Statements, Van Nostrand Reinhold, New York.

Kennedy, W.V. 1984. US and Canadian Experience with Environmental Impact Assessment : Relevance of the Europian Communities?, Zeitschriftfur Umweltpolitik, 7 pp. 339-66.

Khanna, P. 1989. Sustainable Development. Journal of Indian Association for Environmental Management, Vol. 16, No. 1, pp. 6- 19.

Khanna, P. and Kulkarni, V.S. 1992. Policy options for Environmentally sound Technology, Environmentally Sound Technologies for sustainable Development, ATAS Bulletin, Issue No. 7, Spring 1992, United Nations, New York, pp 127-133.

Munn, R.E., 1979. Environmental Impact Assessment : Principles and Procedures, Scope 5 Report, 2 nd Edition, John Wiely, Chichester, England.

UNEP, 1980. Guidelines for Assessing Industrial Environmental Impact and Environmental Criteria for siting of Industry, UNEP Industry and environmental Guidelines Series, Vol. 1, UNEP Industry and Environment Office, Paris.

UNEP 1987. Environmental Law Guidelines and Principles : Environmental Impact Assessment, United Nations Environment Programme, Nairobi.

UNEP, 1988. Environmental Impact Assessment : Basic Procedures for Developing Countries, United Nations Environment Programme, Nairobi.

Wathern, P. 1988. Introduction in Wathern, P. (ed) Environmental Impact Assessment : Theory and Practice, Unwin Hyman, London.

Wood, C., 1994. The Environmental Assessemtn of Plants Programmes and Policies : A comparative Review, Indo-British Workshop on Environmental Impact and Risk Assessment of Petrochemical Industry and Environmental Audit, January 8-10, 1994, Nagpur, India.

CONTENTS

Preface *iii*
Introduction *v*

1. LITERATURE REVIEW 1

1.1. Evolution of EIA World-wide 1
1.2. Evolution of EIA in India 3
1.3. Classification of Environmental Impacts 4
1.4. Project Screening 4
1.4.1. Methodology for screening of Projects 4
1.4.2. Project screening criteria in India 5
1.5. Methodology for Site Selection 6
1.6. EIA Methodologies 7
1.6.1. Introduction 7
1.6.2. Review of EIA Methodologies 8
1.6.2.1. Checklists 8
1.6.2.2. Matrices 12
1.6.2.3. Networks 13
1.6.2.4. Overlays 13
1.6.2.5. Adaptive Environmental Assessment and Management (AEAM) 14
1.6.2.6. Cost-Benefit Analysis (CBA) 14
1.7. Computer Aided EIA 15
1.8. Impact Quantification techniques 15
1.9. Methamatical Model for EIA 16
1.9.1. Concept 16
1.9.2. Air Quality Models 17
1.9.3. Water Quality Models 18
1.9.4. Noise Prediction Models 19
1.10. Indicators of Biological and Socio-economic Environment 21
1.11. Environmental Indices 22
1.12. Enlarged Scope of EIA of Industrial Projects 23
1.13. Conclusions 24

2.	**DEFINITION AND CLASSIFICATION OF WETLANDS**		**25**
	2.1.	Definition	25
	2.2	Classification of Wetlands	26
3.	**BENEFITS OF WETLANDS**		**29**
4.	**REVIEW OF WETLAND MANAGEMENT FRAMEWORKS**		**32**
	4.1.	International Treaties for Wetland Management	32
	4.2.	Regional Initiatives for Wetland Management	33
	4.3.	Status of Wetland Management Programme in India	34
	4.4.	Wetland Area Legislation	38
	4.5.	Wetland Area Administration	39
5.	**INDICATORS FOR WETLAND ASSESSMENT**		**41**
	5.1.	Indicators of Wetland Benefits	41
	5.2.	Indicators for Assessment of Wetland Ecosystem	47
6.	**ENVIRONMENTAL IMPACT ASSESSMENT**		**49**
	6.1.	Concept of EIA	49
	6.2.	Evolution of EIA World-wide	51
	6.3.	Evolution of EIA in India	53
	6.4.	Hierarchy in EIA	54
	6.5.	Major Issue in EIA	54
	6.6.	Classification of Environmental Impacts	56
	6.7.	Project Screening	57
	6.8.	Site selection criteria	60
	6.9.	EIA Methodologies	62
7.	**EIA FOR PROTECTION OF WETLANDS**		**63**
	7.1.	Impacts of Developmental Activities on Wetlands	63
	7.2.	Steps in EIA	65
		7.2.1. Impact Identification	65
		7.2.2. Scoping of Studies	65
		7.2.3. Field Data Collection	65
		7.2.4. Impact Prediction	66
		7.2.5. Impact Evaluation	74
		7.2.6. Impact Mitigation	86
		7.2.7. Post Project Monitoring	87
		7.2.8. Public Participation in EIA	87

WORKSHEETS

No. 1 Identification of wetlands in the study area 94

No. 2 Identification of Project activities likely to affect wetlands 95

No. 3 Identification of potential benefits of wetlands 96

No. 4 Data on wetland indicators 97

No. 5 Matrix for impact assessment of project activities on wetland benefits 98

No. 6 Cost of Mitigation 99

CASE STUDY 1 **100**

EIA of Industrial and Municipal Wastewater Discharges on Wetlands in Calcutta Port Trust Area

CASE STUDY 2. **113**

Keoladeo National Park (Bharatpur, India) — An Ecosystem Study

CASE STUDY 3. **131**

Environmental Impact Assessment of Sundarbans — A Case study

CASE STUDY 4. **139**

EIA of Bhitarkanika Wildlife Sanctuary World-wide Fund for Nature, India

CHAPTER - 1

LITERATURE REVIEW

1.1 EVOLUTION OF EIA WORLDWIDE

United States of America was the first country to assign mandatory status to EIA vide its National Environmental Protection Act (NEPA) of 1969. A host of industrialized countries have since implemented EIA procedures. Canada, Australia, the Netherlands and Japan adopted EIA legislation in 1973, 1974, 1981 and 1984 respectively. In July 1985 the European Community (EC) issued a directive making environmental assessments mandatory for certain categories of projects (Wood, 1994).

Among the developing countries, Columbia was the first Latin American Country to institute a system of EIA in 1974. In Asia and Pacific region, Thailand and Philippines have long- established procedures for EIA. EIA was made mandatory in Sri Lanka in 1984. A manual for EIA was prepared and published in 1988 in Sri Lanka (NBRO, 1988). There is dearth of information on the general situation in Africa, although a number of nations including Rwanda, Botswana and Sudan have experience of EIA (Wathern, 1988).

Bilateral and Multilateral agencies have also recognised the value of EIA as a decision-making tool. The organization for Economic Co-Operation and Development (OECD) issued recommendations on EIA in its constituents states in 1974 and 1979, and for development aid projects in 1986. OECD issued guidelines for good practices in EIA in 1992 (OECD, 1992). United Nations Environment Programme (UNEP) in 1980 provided guidance on EIA of the development proposals (UNEP, 1980) and supported research on EIA in developing countries (Ahmad and Swamy, 1985). UNEP, in 1987 vide the decision

14/25 of the Governing Council, set out goals and principles of EIA for the member countries (UNEP, 1987) and provided guidance on basic procedures for EIA in 1988 (UNEP, 1988).

The World Conservation Strategy pinpointed the need to integrate environmental considerations with development in 1980 (IUCN, 1980). EIA has become an integral part of World Bank Policy (1987), which states that environmental issues must be addressed as part of overall economic policy. In 1989, the World Bank issued the Operational Directive on Environmetal Assessment (O.D. 4.00) which was revised and up-dated on October 1991 (O.D. 4.01). Asian Development Bank in 1990 published guidelines for EIA (ADB, 1990). Importance of EIA was echoed in the Brundtland Report (WCED, 1987), and at United Nations Earth Summit on environment and development held at Rio de Janerio in 1992 (UNCED, 1992).

As foreseen by Garner and O'Riodan (1982) Development of EIA, as a tool for decision making world-over, has emerged through following stages :

* No formal accounting; decisions made on interest group lobbying and engineering feasibility; primary emphasis on economic development.
* Conventional cost-benefit analysis; emphasis an efficiency criterion and engineering feasibility; major concern still economic development.
* Innovative cost-benefit analysis, use of multiple objectives and discount rates, imaginative proxy mechanisms; economic development as one of the objectives
* EIA mainly concerned with describing the repercussions of the proposals on bio-physical processes; economic development still primary objective
* EIA with more attention given to socio-cultural as well as bio-physical systems, economic development principle but not the sole objective
* EIA at two tier level, first to look at generic issues associated with the large projects as a class, second to investigate how an "approved" scheme can best be designed with minimal net social and bio-physical disruption. EIA visualized as a creative participatory environmental management activity.

The summary of evolution of EIA in various countries is presented in Table 1 (Htun, 1988, Wathern, 1988, Wood, 1994).

Table 1. Select List of Activities affecting Wetlands

- Human activities including settlements
- Draining and reclamation for agricultural purposes
- Pollution discharge from agricultural run-off, and domestic and industrial sources
- Over exploitation of fishery resources
- Soil erosion and siltation due to deforestation
- Mining activities and oil exploitation
- Conversion of wetlands to aquaculture ponds
- Use of poisons and explosives in hunting and fishing
- Commercial logging in mangrove and freshwater swam forests

1.2 EVOLUTION OF EIA IN INDIA

Environmental Impact Assessement (EIA) of developmental projects was first introduced in India in 1977-78 when Planning Commission advised the then Department of Science & Technology to take up environmental appraisal of river valley projects. Subsequently, Projects in mining, industry, thermal power, port and harbour sectors were brought under the purview of EIA. At present, the Ministry of Environment and Forests (MEF) is the nodal agency for EIA in India.

The MEF published guidelines for preparation of EIA statements along with questionnaires and checklists for industrial projects (MEF, 1985). Project proponents are required to provide relevant information as indicated in the guidelines alongwith the Environmental Impact Assessement Statement/Environmental Management Plan (EMP). A preliminary scrutiny of the project proposals is made by the technical experts of MEF. After ensuring that the main aspects are covered, EIA reports are placed before the Appraisal Committees of Experts. The Appraisal Committees discusses the impact of the project with the project proponents and, if necessary, site visits are made for on the spot assessment of various environmental aspects. Based on their examination, the Appraisal Committees make recommendations on approval or rejection of the proposal by MEF. The environmental clearance to development projects is subject to implementation of stipulated safeguards under the provisions of Environment (Protection) Act 1986, Forest (Conservation) Act 1980, and other rules and regulations in force.

The MEF on January 27, 1993, brought out draft notification under the Environment (Protection) Act 1986 making environmental clearance mandatory for expansion or modernization of any activity if pollution load is to exceed existing levels, and also for new projects listed in Schedule-I of the notification. The notification was subsequently modified in May 1994 (MEF, 1994).

1.3 CLASSIFICATION OF ENVIRONMENTAL IMPACTS

The term 'impact' and 'effect' are frequently used synonymously in EIA literature, although some researchers have advocated differentiating between natural and man-induced changes, in the biogeophysical environment, effects, from the consequences of these changes, i.e. impacts (Munn, 1979). An impact has both spatial and temporal components and can be described as the change in an environmental parameter over a specified period and within a defined area resulting from a particular activity compared with the situation which would have occurred had the activity not been undertaken.

Impacts can be classified as (Rau and Wooten, 1980) :

* adverse or beneficial
* caused or induced
* primary/secondary/tertiary
* short term/ long term
* reversible/irreversible
* site specific/project specific

In view of the spatial and temporal distribution of the environmental impacts of industrial projects, Agarwal (1992) suggested that the impact of industrial development should be analysed in terms of host, proximate, significantly affected, moderately affected, and slightly affected/unaffected area.

1.4 PROJECT SCREENING

1.4.1 Methodologies for Screening of Projects

EIA procedure needs be applied only to those actions which lead to significant environmental consequence. It is important to establish mechanisms for the selection of actions requiring EIA (Tomlinson, 1984). Screening allows elimination from the review process of all those projects that do not require detailed EIA, thus avoiding unnecessary expense and delays in project clearance.

Screening methods are based on :

- project thresholds
- positive and negative lists
- matrices
- initial environmental examinations

Projects thresholds method relies upon the establishment of threshold values for key features of the project or its environment. If a threshold is exceeded then EIA is required.

Reliance upon one threshold may give rise to an incorrect decisions. It is, therefore, a normal practice to link a series of different threshold together. Threshold, while being simple, may need frequent revision particularly in the light of experience, and inflation when financial criteria are used.

Positive lists are compiled through a review of existing developments, identifying those projects that give rise to significant environmental damage. Lists are one of the simplest approaches to screening. The preparation of lists involves one major problem, viz. individual projects of the same general type or class may have considerable variations in size of plant, process and layout which may give rise to varying environmental consequences. In addition, gaining the acceptance of all parties on the entry of individual project types on particular lists (mandatory positive, intermediate and negative) may be difficult and time consuming.

The united Nations Environmental Programmes (UNEP, 1980) as also the Asian Development Bank (ADB, 1990) have developed questionnaires for the assessment of industrial activities, termed as Initial Environmental Examination (IEE), which provide a simplifed decision tool for screening of projects for EIA. Guidelines for site screening are also published by UNEP (1980).

1.4.2 Project Screening Criteria in India

Notwithstanding the fact that EIA of industrial projects in carried out in India since 1984, no explicit screening criteria were available in India till 1994. The projects appraised by the MEF included (MEF, 1993) :

- Projects which require approval of the Public Investment Board/Planning Commission/Central Electricity authority
- Projects referred to MEF by other Ministeries

- Projects which are sensitive and located in environmentally degraded areas
- Projects of Public sector undertakings of the Government of India where the project cost is more than Rs. 20 Crores

The MEF, vide its notification of May 1994, has made environmental clearance mandatory for expansion or modernization of any activity if pollution load exceed existing levels, and also for new projects listed in Schedule-I of the notification.

1.5 METHODOLOGY FOR SITE SELECTION

The magnitude of environmental impacts of industrial projects is, in most of the cases, site specific. Hence, the selection of site should form an integral part of EIA of industrial projects. However, there are no explicit methodologies documented in literature for site selected. Certain guidelines are provided in the Initial Environmental Examination format of ADB (1990). The World Bank has advised its Task Managers to specifically consider project locations in the categorisation of the projects for futher environmental assessment (World Bank, 1991).

In India, the Ministery of Environment and Forests (MEF, 1985) stipulated that the industrial sites should maintain the following distance from the areas listed below :

* Eologically and/or otherwise sensitive areas : at least 25 kms, the requisite distance may be increased depending on the geo- climatic condition
* Coastal areas : at least 1/2 km from high tide line
* Flood plains of the riverine systems : at least 1/2 km from flood plain or modified flood plain affected by dam in the upstream or by flood control systems
* Transport/communication systems : at least 1/2 km from highways and railways
* Major settlements (more than 3,00,000 population) : distance from settlements is difficult to maintain because of urban sprawl. At the time of siting of the industry if any notified limit of any major settlement is within 50 km, the spatial direction of growth of the settlement for at least a decade must be assessed and the industry shall be sited at least 25 km from the projected growth boundary of the settlement.

The MEF has further stipulated that the following factors must be recognized in siting :

* No forest land shall be converted into non-forest activity for the industry (Forest Conservation Act, 1980).
* No prime agricultural land shall be converted into industrial site
* Within the acquired land the industry must locate itself at the lowest location to remain obscured from general sight
* Land acquired should be sufficiently large to provide space for appropriate treatment of wastewater after maximum possible in house recycle and reuse. Reclaimed (treated) wastewater shall be used for raising green belt and, if possible, for aquaculture.
* The green belt between two adjoining large scale industries shall be one kilometer
* Enough space shall be provided for storage of solid wastes
* Layout and form of the industry must conform to the landscape of the area without affecting the scenic features at that location
* Associated township of the industry must be created at a space having phytographic barrier between the industry and the township.

Ideally, the site for an industrial project should be selected based on the regional carrying capacity (Khanna, *et al.*, 1991) which is defined as the maximum rate of resource consumption and waste discharge that can be sustained indefinitely in a defined planning region without progressively impairing bio-productivity and ecological integrity.

1.6 EIA METHODOLOGIES

1.6.1 Introduction

The identification and assessment of environmental impacts of developmental activities are complex because of the diversity of impacts caused by human interference to the environmental and social systems. Impact identification and assessment requires collection and collation of large amount of diverse data and, most importantly, communicating the final results to the decision makers and members of the public, many of whom are unlikely to be experts in environmental science. It is precisely to help overcome these difficulties that most EIA methods have been devised.

The need for systemization and interdisciplinary studies in EIA led to the development of common structured framework for relating different kind of data. Also, the task of comparing alternative project sites for industries demanded an assessment which allowes direct comparisons to be made between the alternatives. The variety of structured approaches to EIA developed to fulfill these tasks are generally known as EIA methodologies or methods (Bisset, 1984).

1.6.2 Review of EIA Methodologies

Although there is a large number of EIA methodologies which have been developed and used in EIA, the variety is more apparent than real. Nearly all methods are variants of general types which have specific organizing principles in common. These are checklists, matrices, networks, overlays and models. In case of checklists and matrices there are many versions whereas there are fewer examples of networks and models available. All these methodlogies are generic in nature and are adapted to specific type of project assessment such as industrial, water, resources, mining, etc.

1.6.2.1 Checklists

The term checklist covers a variety of methods having widely varying characteristics and degree of complexity. The three basic categories of checklists are : simple checklists, questionnaire checklists and scaling weighing checklists.

Simple Checklists

Simple checklists consist of a list of environmental, economic and social factors which may be affected by specific project actions. These are useful for impact identification. While such a checklist acts as a framework for identifying impacts, additional guidelines are needed to perform the other EIA tasks.

Descriptive Checklists

A comprehensive checklist accompanied by specific guidance on the data requirements, sources of information, and predictive techniques was developed by Schaenman (1976). The guidance allows this checklist to be utilized for impact identification, measurement, and presentation of results. It, however, cannot be used to develop and utilize means of determining the relative importance of different impacts.

Scaling Checklists

The US Forest Service developed a checklist incorporating Threshold of Concern (Sassaman, 1981). This checklist consists of a list of environmental elements or resources such as water quality, wildlife habitat, and air quality accompanied by criteria which express values called "Thresholds of Concern" of these resources which are desirable or which should not be reduced.

The elements, appropriate criteria, and Threshold of Concern values need to be selected for individual projects by those involved in the EIA. Threshold of Concern value for each environmental element is the point at which those assessing a proposal become concerned with the impact. Any impact that exceeds threshold of concern is considered to be significant to decision makers.

Impacts are considered in terms of their duration and reversibility. The checklist assumes that all impacts have equal importance.

Scaling-Weighing Checklists

Condensing information on complex environmental variables into some manageable form is a recurrent problem of assessement. Aggregation with scaling and weighing methods represent a technical fix to this problem (Dee *et al.*, 1973, Solomon *et al.*, 1977).

Scaling weighing checklists have been devised to enable all adverse/beneficial impacts for a single project, or more usefully, alternative projects to be compared in the form of quantitative indices. The result has been the formulation of quasi-mathematical methods in which impacts are weighted in terms of relative importance, transformed into units from a common, notional scale and finally manipulated mathematically to form impact indices. The most well-known of these methods is the Battele Environmental Evaluation System (BEES) employed for water resources projects by Dee *et al.*, (1973). Since then BEES has been adapted for EIA of water quality management plans, highways, nuclear power plants, and other projects.

BEES (Whitman, 1971) is based on scaling weighting checklist consisting of a description of the environmental factors partinent to the project alongwith the instructions for scaling the values of each parameter and assigning importance units. The structure of the BEES is hierarchical in nature to account for different levels of information used in the impact analysis. Four levels of information are used in the BEES, viz.

Level 1 : Most general information - Environmental categories

Level 2 : Intermediate information - Environmental components

Level 3 : Specific information - Environmental parameters

Level 4 : Most specific information - Environmental measurements

This method is essentially concerned with the determination of environmental quality of an area without a project, and then predicting a net positive change, should be project be implemented. This involves predicting the future state of the environment without the project in the same time-scale as that used to predict the project affected environment.

The major features of BEES is that environmental impacts are expressed in commensurate units providing common units for comparison. The steps involved in the development of commnsurate units include transformation of parameter estimates into an environmental quality (EQ) scale, assignment of importance units to the individual parameters (PIU), and the multiplication of scale values by importance values to obtain environmental impact units (EIU).

Environmental quality is measured by the use of value functions for each of the 78 parameters thereby providing a numerical index of overall quality. To achieve this index it is assumed that the quality state of each parameter can be expressed on a scale of 0- 1, where 1 represents highest quality and 0 represents lowest quality. The value function for dissolved oxygen indicates that a level of 10 mg/1 equals a quality score of 1, while 2 mg/1 equals about 0.1. The determination of these quality scores for a variety of environmental components is termed scaling.

To assess the impacts of a project it is necessary to determine the relative importance of various parameters. This is achieved by using experts to assign numerical weights to each parameter. Thousand units are divided between the parameters according to their importance as determined by the experts. To obtain the numerical index for the overall quality, the weightage is multiplied by the quality score for each parameter. The summation of each would then indicate the overall quality state of that area. It is then necessary to predict the likely future state of each parameter assuming the project took place. This may be achieved by mathematical modelling or the use of expert opinion. When the total scores for with and-without project situations are compared, the overall impact of the project can be measured. From such an analysis it would then be possible to select the least damaging alternative. Another benefit of this system is that is has a system of red flags by which serious impacts are highlighted.

By Developing value function curves for the socio-economic conditions BEES has been adapted by workers in various countries (Bisset, 1984). Mangkol (1983) developed an adapted version of BEES through incorporation of impact magnitude (Severity of impacts), prevalence (extent of an impact), duration and frequency (the time element), risk (probability of impact occurrence), importance (significance of impact at the time of EIA work), and mitigation (action that can be taken to reduce or eliminate adverse impacts). This variant of EES involves use of modified value functions to make them flexible to take account of local conditions. The modified value function incorporates maximum and minimum allowable levels for selected environmental parameters. Mangol uses the ratio of beneficial change in environmental impact units of adverse change in environmental impact units as the criterion for project appraisal (Bisset, 1984).

One of the major difficulties with scaling weighing checklists relates to the derivation of weights. Sondheim (1978) attempted to broaden the base of weight allocation, by removing it from those experts who are involved directly in specific EIA studies. In the method proposed by him weighing panel is constitued for each EIA. Each member of the panel produces an individual weighing scheme which is used to produce a composite score for a number of alternative projects.

One important drawback of BEES is its focus on environmental paramters which can be qualified to the extent that there is a great temptation to quantify the unquantifiable, eg. aesthetics. Further, subjective views incorporated in EES are representative of a very restricted population, namely experts (Bisset, 1984).

Many subjective elements are subsumed within both the weighing scheme and the value functions. In effect, the basis for decision is created by the method. The preferred option and, hence, the only decision that logically can be taken is one with the highest score for environmental quality.

BEES is complex to operate and any Environmetal Impact Statement (EIS) prepared using this or a similar method would not be comprehended easily by non-experts. Not only would the technical information on impacts needs to be understood, but also the principles of the method need to be comprehended. Finally, the compexity of this approach results in requirements of large manpower, time and resource requirements especially when determining the value functions.

Despite these drawbacks, BEES is regarded as the most suitable method to aggregate impacts of a developmental project and present them to the decision makers.

1.6.2.2 Matrices

Matrix methods are two-dimensional checklists in which possible project activities are established along one axis, with potentially impacted environmental characteristics or conditions along the other. Thus the cause-effect relationships between specific activities and impacts are identified in matrix methods.

Leopold *et al.* (1971) were the first to suggest the use of a matrix for EIA. The Leopold matrix is complex. A total of 8800 cells result from 88 environmental parameters along one ax is and 100 developmental characteristics along the other. The matrix format is ideally suited for impact identification (Munn, 1979).

The Leopold matrix is also useful to present the results of an appraisal. This is achieved by incorporating guidelines to characterise impacts in terms of magnitude and importance on a common 1-10 scale, where 1 is least magnitude or importance, and 10 the greatest. The magnitude of an impact is taken to be an expression of its scale, e.g. the geographical area of the impact. The Score for importance may, however, be different. Importance refers to the significance of the impact. If a visual impact were to occur in an area of poor landscape quality then a score of only 2 or 3 may be awarded instead of 8 or 9 in an area of high quality.

Leopold *et al.* recommend that scores for magnitude and importance should be included in the appropriate cell of the matrix representing a likely impact. The cell should be bisected by a diagonal line with the score for magnitude being placed in the top left-hand corner. The score for importance is placed in the bottom right-hand corner. These scores can be accompanied by a plus sign (+) to indicate a beneficial effect. A completed matrix would consist of a number of cells containing two numerical scores and, in some cases, a plus sign.

The usefulness of a Leopold type matrix has been demonstrated in the assessment of exploratory drilling sites in Antartica (Parker and Howard, 1977). Matrices were used to assess the impacts of drilling at alternative sites, and to identify the location where drilling could take place with minimum environmental disturbance. Twenty matrices were prepared to identify the 'best' site for drilling.

Despite the demonstration of the usefulness of Leopold-type matrices, they pose serious theoretical and practical limitations. Those assessing a project have to structure their thoughts by mentally linking a target component and a development activity in order to ascertain whether an impact is likely. It is then necessary to consider the next component in a similar manner. Thus, impacts are identified by a series of discrete, two-way linkages between activities and components of the environment, thereby indicating the likely direct impacts.

1.6.2.3 Networks

The first EIA network was developed by Sorensen in 1971 to aid planners reconcile conflicting land-uses in a section of Californian coastal zone (Bisset, 1984).

Network approaches expand the concept of a matrix by introducing a cause-condition-effect relation that allwos identification of cumulative or indirect effects not adequately explained through simple cause effects sequences represented by matrices. Networks, thus, recognize that a project action may tirgger a series of impacts.

Network methods are based on an explicit recognition that the consequences of an action can have many ramifications for environmental and social systems. Networks provide an integrative framework for impact identification and assessment which recognizes the nature of complex web of interrelationships which characterize both environmental and social systems, and the connection between them.

Network methods are not useful in impact prediction or assessment, and rely heavily on the expertise and local knowledge of persons involved in EIA. Further, for a complex project such as industrial development, the cause-condition-effect network can be unwieldy visual display.

1.6.2.4 Overlays

Overlays mappings have a long history of use in environmental planning being ideally suited for the consideration of spatial aspects. Their use in impact analysis pre-dates NEPA (McHarg, 1968). The Technique relies on a set of maps of environmental characteristics (physical, biological, socioeconomic, etc.) of a project area. These maps are overlaid to produce a composite characterization of the regional environment. Impacts are identified by noting the impacted environmental characteristics within the project boundaries.

The simple method of visually representing individual impacts and combinations of impacts has a number of advantages. The results from application of these overlay methodology are easily understood. Most importantly, it is an excellent method for showing spatial distribution of impacts. With this information, it is relatively easy to relate individual impacts and the total aggregate impact of a project.

The method also allows the determination of distribution of beneficial and adverse impacts.

There are a number of disadvantages to manual overlays. Interpretation of more than twelve overlays at one time is often difficult. This means that only limited number of impacts can be considered as each impact requires separate transparency. This constraint can be overcome by the use of computers. The computerised overlays have been used for assessing a number of developments (Doorley and Newkirk, 1976).

Experience with the overlay methodology indicates that it is most useful in assessing alternative routes for linear developments, such as pipelines, highways and transmission lines. Composite displays enable the impacts of routes to be assessed also can show routes which will have least environmental impact. Therefore, overlays are very useful 'search' mechanisms.

1.6.2.5 Adaptive Environmental Assessment and Management (AEAM)

Systems analysts have evolved an approach to environmental impact assessment and management referred to as adaptive Environment Assessment and Management (AEAM) (Holling, 1978) which combines various simulation models to predict impacts. The AEAM approach involves small interdisciplinary teams interacting through modelling workshops over relatively short period to predict impacts and evaluate alternatives including management measures. The models, however, will only be as accurate and comprehensive as the data available.

1.6.2.6 Cost-Benefit Analysis (CBA)

Recognize the fact that the traditional approaches towards EIA do not lend themselves to the integration of environmental concerned with the overall planning process, UNEP proposed an approach dealing with the evaluation of environmental impacts in monetary units to facilitate easy comparison with other costs and benefits of the projects (UNEP, 1980).

The CBA is not a complete EIA methodology but comes into the EIA process only after the identification and prediction steps have been performed. This approach therefore, must be used with other EIA methodologies.

The CBA approach differs from the traditional EIA in that a separate document is not prepared as an EIS. Instead, environmental personnel work alongside economists and engineers througout the entire planning process. Duplication of efforts is thus eliminated and costs of feasibility studies are reduced. Most importantly, the decision maker, when reviewing the project, would not view environmental considerations as separate or auxillary to economic development. Although developing countries may be far from putting this approach into practice, it is a goal to work towards for those concerned with balancing environment and development.

1.7 COMPUTER AIDED EIA

Use of computer in EIA, with a few exceptions, has been restricted to development of software for storage and retrieval of environmental data, and software for predictive modelling.

Urban *et al.*, (1975) developed a computer aided assessment system using matrix approach to identify potential environmental impacts associated with army activities in the areas of training, research and development, construction, real-estate acquisition, and industrial activities.

Krauskopf and Bunde (1972) developed a computer modelling process employing overlay technique via computer mapping for highway- route alternatives. Data on environment characteristics are collected and stored in the computer on a grid system of 1 km square cells. The programme identifies the route of least impact.

Luhar and khanna (1988) developed a methodology for computer aided rapid EIA. The methodology consists of a predefined set of environmental predictors for baseline data collection, uses RAM model of USEPA for prediction of air quality, simple diffusion equations for predicting thermal pollution in water, and appropriate models for estimation of noise levels. The methodology and index indicators such as importance value and census index for biology environment, and index of qualitative variation and dependency ratio for socio-economic environment. Impacts are evaluated using BEES.

The research in computer aided EIA, so far, lacks the use of comprehensive methodology for identification of impacts, identification and use of appropriate prediction models, and evaluation of impacts using predictors relevant to the type of project.

1.8 IMPACT QUANTIFICATION TECHNIQUES

The step in EIA which requires the greatest degree of scientific application is the prediction of environmental impacts. This step involves projecting the baseline environmental setting into the future, with and without the project, and then performing necessay calculations for predicting real impacts of the proposed development. The mathematical models for prediction of impact on air, noise and water environment are well established. Indices need to be used for assessing biological and socio-economic environment. The impact is measured as change in these indices. Indices also can be used for aggregation and communication of Impacts.

1.9 MATHEMATICAL MODELS FOR EIA

1.9.1 Concept

Models are simplified representations of reality and can be subdivided into three main classes :

* a scaled - down copy of physical object such as building
* a mathematical represenation of a physical or biological process, eg. of the spread of pollution from a stack or the movement of a weather disturbance across a region.
* an exploratory representation of complex relationships amongst physical, biological, and socio-economic factors or indicators, some quantitative others qualitative.

Mathematical models can further be classified as :

- Steady state models - where the system does not vary with time. The inputs to the model are fixed and consequently the system eventually reaches some equilibrium condition. Steady state models are simplistic and have small data requirements.
- Dynamic models - where the system varies with time due to changing conditions or due to chaging imputs. Dynamic models are more difficult to formulate and require larger amounts of data. They also require larger computing time.
- Deterministic models - where there is a fixed relationship between the input and output. All the relationships in such a model are rigidly determined, and the input and output are similarly assumed to be error free.
- Stochastic models - which allow for random fluctuations in the system due to variations in the input parameters, variations in the state of the system coefficients, or errors in output measurements. The variations are introduced by fixing the mean value of a parameter or coefficient together with the standard deviation. Data requirements for such a model are obviously greater than the equivalent deterministic model.

Mathematical model is the description of the behavior of a system in quantitative terms. It is approximate description of reality and is by no means a substitution for observing the real behaviour. Modelling exercise should be done with a clear end use in mind. In fact, well defined end use will dictate the need for modelling (Modak, 1987).

1.9.2 Air Quality Models

Air quality models predict the ground level concentrations of pollutants due to specified emission sources. The processes which govern the fate of pollutants in the atmosphere include transportation by wind and diffusion due to turbulance. Exit velocity, emission temperature, removal of pollutants through processes such as chemical transformations, wet deposition, dry deposition, and aerodynamic effects of natural and manmade terrain features also govern the dispersion of pollutants. It is difficult to incorporate all these phenomena in a single model. Gnerally, a basic transport and diffusion model is formulated which is then modified to include other processes through sub-models of air chemistry, meteorological interactions etc. Air quality models can be classified based on temporal resolution, sources, receptors and mathematical techniques.

Based on temporal resolution, air quality models can be classified as short to medium range models, and long range models. Short range (upto about 10 km) to medium range (upto about 30 km) models are applied to areas closer to the source. Long range models examine the fate of pollutants which travel hundreds or thousands of kilometers, and generally consider the physical processes of dry and wet pollutant deposition and chemical changes. Short-range models are used mainly for hazard determination during emergencies, or for assessing impacts of new sources and their compliance with air quality standards. Long range models are used for assessing impacts of distant sources, often in other countries. In EIA of industrial projects, short-range models are more relevant.

Mathematical techniques in air quality models include empirical, semi-empirical, and mass conservation approaches. The most commonly used air quality models are based on Gaussian Plume Model (GPM).

Gaussian model was established in 1960s based on the work carried out by Pasquill and Gifford (Rau & Wooten, 1980). The model assumes normal distributions of pollutants along vertical and horizontal perpendicular to the direction of wind. It permits assessments of continuous or instantaneous release of pollutant, with or without a linear reaction rate or decay. GPM is a semi-empirical and semi-theoretical in nature.

The extentions of the basic Gaussian model include the following features :

* pollution reflection at the ground and at the inversion lid
* introduction of different sources (point, line, area)
* linear reaction or decay rate, washout by rain, settling of particles, uptake by vegetation or water
* topographic effects
* lake or sea breeze
* temperol and spacial variations in meteorological conditions

The software packages available from United State Environmental Protection Agency (USEPA), which are based on GPM, under the acronym UNAMAP. In 1970s, UNAMAP models required mainframe computers. In late 1980s, Trinity consultants translated a number of UNAMAP models for IBM PC. In some cases, Trinity also developed interactive data entry programmes and graphics (Reiss, 1985).

1.9.3 Water Quality Models

Rivers have traditionally been used for the disposal of domestic and industrial wastewaters. This results in undesirable impacts on aquatic flora and fauna. The majority of these changes are brought about by the discharge of organic matter (BOD) resulting in lowering in the concentration of dissolved oxygen (DO) in the receiving water. Pollution of rivers is also caused by the discharge of toxic substances, which may break down due to chemcial or bacterial action (non-conservative) or may be resistent to breakdown (conservative). Other problems arise due to discharge of inorganic nutrients causing excessive algal growth. In all these situations it is important to be able to relate the rate of discharge of pollutant to resulting concentrations in the receiver water.

An important application of mathematical modelling is to obtain a continuous profile of water quality out of observed sparse data. Once the continuous profile is obtained, it is possible to relocate or rationalize the water quality monitoring networks. Continuous profile of water quality could also be obtained for different conditions where response of water quality system could be extrapolated (simulation). Surface water quality models have been used over several decades to determine waste treatment levels and effluent standards so that the receiving streams would meet the water quality criteria for their best designated usages.

The assumptions pertaining to the mixing of pollutants in river system dictate the spacial dimensionality of the model. Although all real physicla systems are three-dimensional, sufficient accuracy may be obtained in many river systems by modelling only one or two dimensions (Beck, 1987). One dimensional models assume complete mixing in the vertical and lateral directions. Two dimensional models may assume either uniform lateral mixing, as in stratified estuaries, or vertical mixing as in relatively shallow and wide rivers. In view of availability and wider acceptibility of 1-D water quality models, the present work reviews only 1-D water quality models.

Various water quality models have been developed over the years, beginning with the classic work on BOD/DO models by Streeter and Phelps in the 1920s (Beck, 1987). This laid the basis for modelling the biochemical kinetics of organic matter breakdown. Subsequent research has concentrated on the hydrodynamic aspects - advection and diffusion - alongwith stochastic and statistical models, and refinement of kinetic models.

Streeter & Phelps carried out work on impact of point sources of pollution and natural purification processes in the Ohio River. The method used simplistic approach of taking biochemical oxygen demand (BOD) loads as the major depleter of the dissolved oxygen (DO) and reaeration (transfer of atmospheric oxygen from air to water at the air water interface) of the river as the source of oxygen. The saturation deficit of the dissolved oxygen is considered as the driving force the re-aeration phenomenon. The model used steady state condition, in which the rate of dissolved oxygen depletion was assumed to be equivalent to the rate of re-aeration.

Most of the water quality models in actual use today are extensions of two fairly simple equations proposed by Streeter and Phelpe (Loucks, 1981, and Thomann, 1982). Often used with these BOD-DO models are other first exponential decay, dilution, and sedimentation models for conservation and non-conservative substances. Relatively recently complex multiparameter water quality models have been proposed and applied to predict more accurately the physical, chemical and biological interactions of many constituents and organisms found in natural water bodies. These multi-constituent water quality simulation models generally require more data and computer time but they also provide detailed and comprehensive information on the quantity and quality of water resulting from various water and land management policies.

In the past two decades there has been an increasing emphasis on the effects of various constituents, specially nutrients, on the aquatic ecosystem, i.e., on the production of phytoplankton, zooplankton, fish and other trophic levels within the natural water bodies Typical of many of the operational aquatic ecosystem simulation models are QUAL series of models.

Temporal/Overall Model for Catchment (TOMCAT), developed by the Thames Water Authorities, United Kingdom, is another versatile model for 1-dimensional modelling of rivers. The model takes into account the diurnal variations in the wastewater and river flows with the help of Monte Carlo Simulation. The process simulated by TOMCAT include thermal transfer, natural purification comprising carbonaceous organics oxidations, oxidation of ammoniacal nitrogen (Nitrification), and oxygen balance considering these processes as sinks, and reaeration as the source of dissolved oxygen (Joshi, 1993).

Recently, Modak *et al.*, (1989) developed 1-D water quality simulation and waste load allocation model, acronymed STREAM-1. The model incorporates nitrogenous BOD pointload and non-point carbonaceous BOD in the classic Streeter-Phelps equation. The major contribution of the model relation to the use of random search technique for calibration of model parameters based on the field data.

1.9.4 Noise Prediction Models

The term noise is defined as unwanted and undesirable sound. Mathematical basis for noise prediction (Sound wave divergence) is well unserstood (Rau and Wooten, 1980). Three basic elements involved in the study of noise predictions are the source, the receptor, and the transmission path. The sources of noise may be categorised as mobile and stationary sources; point, line and area sources; continuous, intermittent and implusive sources etc.

In open space sound level diminishes as the distance increases due to the geometric dispersion of the sound power. The transmission path from source to receptor is characterised by the properties of the medium, i.e air, and the presence of scatterers, viz. walls, trees, vegetation etc. Noise is attenuated during transmission due to atmospheric absorption, scatteered by natural and artificial barriers, and absorbed due to ground cover. The sound energy reaching a receptor may be due to a number of sources of different characteristics.

The net energy reaching a receptor from a number of sources may be computed by logarithmic addition of the noise level at the receptor due to all the source independently.

Generation of traffic noise varies according to volume of traffic, types of vehicles comprising the steam and their modes of operation. Once the noise is generated the resulting noise field depends upon propagation conditions such as road alignment, geometry, land topography, screening by obstacles and reflection from surfaces. Mathematical description of these processes and the resulting development of prediction techniques are used widely for assessment of traffic noise, planning and design of roads and adjoining landuse.

Federal Highway Administration (FHWA) of USA developed a model increase in noise levels due to traffic (FHWA, 1972). The model computes hourly equivalent noise level increase due to automobiles, medium and heavy trucks separately then adds these levels logarithemically. The model takes into account vehicle type, speed, number of vehicle passing per hour, perpendicular distance from the center line of the traffic lane to receptor, absorption coefficient of ground and vegetation.

Impact on noise levels due to industrial point sources is fairly easy to compute. However, in complex situations, and consideration of barriers require use of computers. Commercial software packages for noise level predictions due to point sources are not widely available.

1.10 INDICATORS OF BIOLOGICAL AND SOCIO-ECONOMIC ENVIRONMENT

The complexity and variability of biological and socio-economic systems make precise quantitative predictions of impact of industrial development impossible (Rau and Wooten, 1981). Hence, impact on biological and socio-economic environment is quantified in terms of appropriate indicators.

The impacts of Industrial project on socio-economic environment can be assessed in terms of Quality of Life (QOL). Different agencies have employed indices to measure quality of life (QOL) in terms of political, economic, social, physical, and health and ambient environmental quality issues. These indices mainly vary in terms of parameteric selection for computation of QOL.

According to USEFA, QOL is defined as a function between objective conditions and subjective attitudes involving a defined area of concern (EPA, 1974). The computation of quality of life involves following stemp :

* Computation of objective QOL index

$$QOL_o = \sum_{i-1}^{m} QI_i \times W$$

QOL_o = Objective QOL index

QI_i = Objective Quality Index for i^{th} factor

W = Weight of the ith factor

m = No. of factors

* Computation of subjective QOL index

$$QOL_s = 1/P \sum_{j=1}^{p} \sum_{i=1}^{m} QI_{ij} \times W$$

QOL_s = Subjective QOL index

QI_s = Subjective Quality index (VFC) for i^{th} factor

W = Weight of the ith factor

m = No. of Factors

P = Sample Population Size

* Computation of aggregate QOL index

$$QOL = \frac{QOL_o + QOL_s}{2}$$

1.11 ENVIRONMENTAL INDICES

Much of the initial research on environmental indices was carried out in early 1970s to measure progress towards environmental goals and pollution control targets (Ott,. 1978). These were conceived as tools to describe the level of environmental quality in a particular medium for a particular region. Interregional comparisions were an important focus of the work.

Traditionally, environmental indices have been closely linked to environmental monitoring with the intent to provide insight into environmental conditions, and as yardstick to judge the effectiveness of environmental regulatory programmes.

There are four stages in the development of an environmental index :

* Parameter selection
* Development of value function curves/scaling technique
* Assigning parameter importance units (weights)
* Selection of appropriate aggregation function

1.12 ENLARGED SCOPE OF EIA OF INDUSTRIAL PROJECTS

In EIA of industrial projects, the manufacturing process is considered as a black-box. The traditional focuss on pollution control through end of the pipe (EOP) treatment which allows wasteful use of resources and then consumes further resources to solve the environmental problems in a particular medium. End of the pipe control technologies, more often than not, transfer pollutants from one environmental medium to another, and consume resources out of proportion to the accrued benefits (Kulkarni *et al.*, 1991).

Future raw material and energy scenarios, the impact that the industry and its products have on the natural resource base and environmental quality. and the necessary thrust being given to industrial growth in Indian warrant a comprehensive strategy to deal with environmental and economic problems of the industry.

As new industries come up to meet developmental imperatives, it will be necessary to impose more stringent emission standards progressively to maintain acceptable levels of environmental quality. Hence, the options for environmental management in industry sector include, on the one hand, reactive control measures such as end-of the pipe (EOP) treatment technologies and media-specific regulations for waste discharges, and on the other, anticipative and preventive strategies such as adoption of cleaner technologies (CT) of production and integrated planning based on considerations of regional carrying capacity (Khanna and Kulkarni, 1992).

While in theory it is agreed that the most appropriate stage where EIA of industrial project should begin is the selection of manufaturing technology, no such case studies are available in the documented literature.

Incorporation of CTs in EMPs is considerably impeded by lack of information exchange between various interest groups on opportunities for pollution prevention. A meaningful data base accessible through on-line information retrieval system on availability and accessibility of CTs and their economic viability, and suitability to local environment, skills and raw materials does not exist. The available databases lack crucial information on possible savings in raw material consumption and reduction in pollution control costs through adoption of CTs (Khanna and Kulkarni, 1994).

1.13 CONCLUSION

While EIA is in practice in various countries since early 1970s, R & D endeavour in development of methodologies for EIA has been limited. This is so as many EIA practioners conceive it as an exercise involving technical commonsense and involving minimum effort on quantification of impacts.

The crucial step in EIA, screening and impact identification, is aided with tools such as positive lists and checklists. This leaves substantial margin for objective decision making. Further, the checklists documented in the literature are useful in identification of primary impacts. Checklists fail to guide the project team in delineation of data requirements and identification of analysis tools.

The incorporation of environmental concerns in the process of site selection is presently enabled thorugh extention of matrices for project level EIA. These matrices fail to include carrying capacity attributes in site selection.

The mathematical models widely used for prediction of impacts on air and water quality were developed by USEPA as regulatory tools to achieve pollution control targets. These models were developed to handle specific situations. These packages are not user-friendly, and the output needs expert interpretation for use in EIA. Commercial packages for prediction of occupational noise levels are not yet available.

The Environmental Evaluation System (EES) developed by Dee *et al.*, (1973) is considered as a combursome methodology. The application of EES is thus rarely reported in literature. The methodology can be suitably adapted to circumvent the documented limitations through a combination of features in BEES and Leopold matrix.

The EIA porject team needs to assesses subjectivity in assigning weights in EES.

The present research addresses itself to the development of software on personal computer platform to bridge these glaring gaps in the theory and practice of EIA.

CHAPTER - 2

DEFINITION AND CLASSIFICATION OF WETLANDS

2.1 DEFINITION

Wetlands are unique ecosystems which occupy transitional zone between permanently wet and generally dry environments and share characteristics of both these environments.

There are more than fifty definitions of wetland currently in use (Dugan, 1990). Some commonly used definitions are:

* Wetlands are submerged or water-saturated lands, both natural and man-made, permanent or temporary, with water that is static or flowing, fresh, brackish or salty, including areas of marine water, the depth of which at low tide does not exceed six meters (IUCN, 1971).
* Wetlands are areas dominated by herbaceous macrophytes, the production of which takes place predominantly in the aerial environment above the water level while the plants are supplied with amounts of water that would be excessive for most other higher plants (International Biosphere Programme, 1972).
* Wetlands are ecological structures in succession from open water to dry land and vice versa, occurring at sites situated as a rule between the highest and lowest water levels where the flooding or water logging of the soil is of substantial ecological significance (Fifth General Assembly of International Biological Programme (1972).

* Wetlands are areas that at least periodically supports hydrophytes, where the subsoil is predominantly undrained hydric soil and the substrate is non-soil and is saturated by water or covered by water at some time during each growing season (Cowardin et al., 1979).
* Wetlands includes areas of marsh, fen, peatland or water regardless of degree of salinity (natural or artificial, permanent or temporary, with static or flowing water), including marine waters upto 6 m. in depth at low tide (UNESCO, 1982)
* Wetlands are areas where water table is at or near surface, or areas saturated for long enough period to promote wetland or hydric processes (Mitsch and Grosselink, 1986)

2.2 CLASSIFICATION OF WETLANDS

There are numerous wetland typologies in use around the world. The best known of these is perhaphs that produced for the United States Department of the Interior (Cowardin et al., 1979). This system classifies wetlands into five systems - marine, estuarine, riverine, lacustrine and palustrine at the first level. These are further sub-divided into 120 sub-classes. However, this classification does not include man-made wetlands.

Table - 2. Classification of Wetlands

Type	Description
Swamp	Swamps is a general term used to describe all kinds of vegetated wetalnd areas. It includes freshwater, saline and brackish areas. Characteristicly, these areas inndated by water for much, if not all, of the year. This often results in permanently water logged soil conditions.
* Swamp Forest - Peat Swamp Forest - Other Swamp Forest	Swamp forests include all forested swamp lands. Peat swamp forests are the forested lands which occur on peat soils.
* Non-Forested Swamp - Overflow Wetlands - Other Wetlands	Other swamp forests are mainly freshwater swampforest. These are usually found on seasonally or permanently flooded alluvial soil characterised by an organic content less than 35%. There may be thin layer of soil which resembles peat. The most common occurences of this formation are as riverain wetland forest and coastal plains.

	Non-forested swamps are areas with grasses and/or sedges and sometimes with areas of open water. Overflow wetlands occur in river floodplains, and are usually fed by overflow water from rivers. The vegetation may be herbaceous (grasses and sedges), floating mats or scrub. Other non-forested swamps are areas of shallow water and include areas fed by ground water, lake edge wetlands and some tidal wetlands.
Mangroves	Mangroves are coastal saline tidal forests.
Coral	These are cral reefs (formations) and include fringing reefs, atrolls and barrier reefs.
Seagrass and Seaweed	These areas form extensive beds in intertidal and subtidal areas.
Lakes	Includes small and large lakes, dams, reserviors and ponds.
Estuaries	This is part of river where there is sometimes or always brackisk or salt water and where tidal influence in significant.
Rivers * Rivers * River Pools	Includes river pools, cataracts and waterfalls. This category also includes small river-fed ponds closely associated with river systems.
Rice Fields * Tidally Irrigated * Non-Tidally Irrigated - Rainfed - Non-Rainfed	These are man-made wetlands under rice cultivation.
Fishponds/Aquaculture	Includes brackish and freshwater fish and shrimp breeding ponds
Salt Pans	These are man-made wetlands where saline water is allowed to evaporate, forming salt crystals which are then harvested.

Source : Howe et al. (1991)

The classification system developed by the Asian Wetland Bureau is based on biophysical characteristics and use into 3000 types. However, the classification employs terminology which is commonly used within scientific rather than the general community. Hence its utility for impact assessment on wetlands will be limited.

Howe et al. (1991) have developed a far simpler scheme of wetland classification for use in scoping of environmental impact assessment study of projects affecting wetlands, which and is presented in Table 2. This scheme has been followed in this manual for environmental impact assessment.

CHAPTER - 3

BENEFITS OF WETLANDS

Potential benefits associated with wetlands can be categorized based on their functions, uses and attributes (Howe et al., 1991).

Functions of wetland are services provided such as reduction in air- or water- borne pollutants by biophysical processes occurring within the wetland.

Uses involve direct physical interaction with the natural area, usually resulting in the extraction of products of some type.

Attributes are those aspects of wetland which, whilst not yielding either a physical service or a good, provide for some psychological aspects of human needs such as cultural, heritage and aesthetic characteristics.

Summary of benefits associated with various types of wetlands are presented in Table 3.

Table 3. Potential Benefits of Wetlands

Potential Benefits	Wetland Type										
	Swamps		Man-groves	Coral Reefs	Seagrass and Seaweed	Lakes	Estuaries	Rivers	Rice fields	Aqua-culture	Salt Pans
	Swamp Forest	Non-Forseted Swamps									
Functions											
Flood mitigation	*	*				*	*	*	*	*	
Prevention of intrusion of saline waters	*					*		*			
Storm protection	*	*	*	*	*		*			*	*
Sediment removal	*	*	*		*	*	*	*	*		
Nutrient removal	*	*	*	*	*	*	*	*	*		
Toxicant removal	*	*	*		*	*	*	*	*		
Groundwater recharge	*	*				*			*		
Groundwater discharge	*	*				*					
Erosion mitigation		*	*		*	*				*	
Nutrient export	*	*	*	*	*		*		*	*	
Wildlife habitat	*	*	*	*			*		*		
Fish habitat	*	*	*	*	*		*		*		
Toxicant export										*	

Table 3 contd...

Uses											
Forestry	*		*								
Agriculture	*	*				*		*	*		
Forage production		*				*					
Recreation/tourism	*	*	*	*		*	*	*			
Transport medium	*	*				*	*	*			
Water supply	*	*				*	*	*			
Mineral production	*			*		*		*			*
Pest production	*	*	*					*			
Wildlife production	*	*	*	*		*		*	*		
Fish production	*	*	*	*	*	*	*	*	*		
Aquaculture		*	*	*		*	*	*		*	
Research site	*	*	*	*	*	*	*	*			
Education site	*	*	*	*	*	*	*	*			
Fertilizer production						*					
Energy production	*		*				*	*			
Attributes											+
Biological diversity	*	*	*	*	*	*	*	*			
Cultural or historic value	*	*	*	*	*	*	*	*			
Aesthetics value	*	*	*	*	*	*	*	*			
Wilderness value	*	*	*	*	*	*	*	*			

CHAPTER - 4

REVIEW OF WETLAND MANAGEMENT FRAMEWORKS

4.1 INTERNATIONAL TREATIES FOR WETLAND MANAGEMENT

Wetlands are truly internationally important habitats and impacts on them can occur through events at considerable distance from wetland areas, often beyond national boundaries. Much of the wetland fauna are migratory species whose conservation and management require international cooperation. Realizing the rapid deterioration and loss of wetlands throughout the world, the Convention on Wetlands of International Importance especially as Waterfowl Habitat, was adopted at the city of Ramsar in Iran in February, 1971. The Convention, popularly known as Ramsar Convention, is an intergovernmental treaty which provides the framework for international cooperation for the conservation of wetland habitats. The Convention follows an extremely broad approach in determining the wetland habitats which come under its aegis. These include rivers, lakes, coastal zones, areas of marsh, fen, peatlands and others.

The Convention came into force in December, 1975 and has now 83 Contracting Parties from all over the world. The Convention has twelve articles which deal with various aspects of wetlands, including their definition, criteria for designation of wetlands, obligations and responsibilities of Contracting Parties, wise-use of wetlands, establishing nature reserves, research, monitoring, manage- ment of wetland species, international cooperation, transboundary wetland issues, etc.

The main obligation of the Governments joining the Ramsar Convention are:

* Designating at least one wetland for inclusion in the list of Wetlands of International Importance
* Promoting wise-use of wetlands
* Consulting each other about implementing obligations arising from the Convention, especially, but not exclusively, in the case of shared wetlands or water systems
* Creating wetland reserves

The United Nations Conference on Environment and Development (1992) suggested close collaboration between Ramsar Convention and the Convention on Biological Diversity for conservation of biodiversity of wetlands.

The other major international treaties related to wetlands include:

* The Convention on International Trade in Endangered Species of Wild Flora and Fauna (CITES)
* Convention on Conservation of Migratory Species of Wild Animals (The Bonn Convention)
* The Convention on Protection of World Cultural and Natural Heritage
* The Convention on Climate Change

4.2 REGIONAL INITIATIVES FOR WETLAND MANAGEMENT

The Ramsar Convention, inter alia, highlights the need for regional cooperation for effective conservation and wise use of wetlands. Such cooperation among the Asian countries carries an even greater potential in view of the vast and diverse wetland resources in the region. Seven of the world's top twenty five biologically richest countries are in Asia.

In Asia, Regional meetings on wetlands were held at Karachi in 1991, Islamabad in 1992, Kushiro in 1992 and a sub-regional meeting in Bogor and Pulau Rambut, Indonesia in 1994. The Karachi meeting focused on conservation of wetlands in South and West Asia and an action plan was formulated and recommended to eleven countries in Asian region for implementation. Subsequent to this, the Islamabad meeting deliberated on strengthening regional networking to promote Ramsar Convention in the region. The Kushiro meeting addressed crucial issues relating to wise use of wetlands in Asia. The sub-regional meeting held at Bogor, Indonesia focused on strengthening of institutional mechanism for protection and wise use of wetlands in South East Asia.

Wise use of Wetlands

Article 3.1 of Ramsar Convention demonstrates a country's commitment to wise use of wetlands in its territory. The wise use concept is very closely related to the concept of sustainable development. It was defined at the Ragina Conference held in 1987 which states that "the wise use of wetlands is their sustainable utilization for the benefit of mankind in a way compatible with the maintenance of the natural properties of the ecosystem". It clearly indicates that the Ramsar Convention is concerned not only with protection of wetlands resources but also with their rational use for the benefit of mankind.

In Asia, as elsewhere, local communities are repository of knowledge on wetlands and have played a significant role in their conservation over the millennium. It would be worthwile to share their experience in this regard. The process of learning from local communities could also be shared among the countries of the region. The role of NGOs, too would be crucial for creating awareness and public participation.

Source: Concept Paper for Asian Regional Meeting of the Contracting Parties of the Ramsar Convention, March 23-25, 1995, New Delhi, India.

The Asian Ramsar Regional meeting was organized at Delhi in March 1995 to strengthen regional networking for wise use of wetlands. The main issues for discussion in this meeting were wise use of wetlands, conservation of listed sites and international cooperation.

4.3 STATUS OF WETLAND MANAGEMENT PROGRAMME IN INDIA

Recognizing the importance of wetlands, a scheme was introduced in the VII Five Year Plan (1987-92) for conservation of wetland ecosystem. A National Committee on Wetlands, Mangroves and Coral Reefs has been constituted with the Secretary, Ministry of Environment and Forests (MEF) as Chairman, in 1987. The Committee was reconstituted in 1990. The Committee advises the

Government on policy guidelines for implementing programmes of conservation management and research on wetlands. The broad components of the management action plan of a wetland include survey and demarcation, notification, wildlife conservation, development of avifauna and fisheries, weed control, pollution abatement, water quality management, protection, environmental awareness etc. State level steering committees have also been constituted for formulation and implementation of management action plans.

So far 21 wetlands have been identified in India for intensive conservation and management purposes. The list of wetlands identified for conservation is presented in Table 4.

Table - 4. List of Wetlands in India Identified for Conservation and Management by the Ministry of Environment and Forests

Sr. No.	Wetland	State
1	Kolleru	Andhra Pradesh
2	Wular	Jammu & Kashmir
3	Chilka	Orissa
4	Loktak	Manipur
5	Bhoj	Madhya Pradesh
6	Sambhar	Rajsthan
7	Asthamudi	Kerala
8	Harike	Punjab
9	Ujni	Maharashtra
10	Sukhana	Chandigarh
11	Sasthamkotta	Kerala
12	Renuka	Himachal Pradesh
13	Kabar	Bihar
14	Nalsarovar	Gujrat
15	Kanjli	Punjab
16	Keoladeo Ghana National Park	Rajasthan
17	Tse Morari	Jammu & Kashmir
18	Pongdam Lake	Himachal Pradesh
19	Chandratalal Lake	Himachal Pradesh
20	Ropar	Punjab
21	East Calcutta Wetland	West Bengal

Source : Wetlands of India - A Directory, Ministry of Environment and Forests, New Delhi, 1990; MEF Annual Report 1993-94

India is a signatory to Ramsar convention. The following six wetlands have been designated as wetlands of international importance under the convention :

* Chilka (Orissa)
* Keoladeo Ghana National Park (Rajasthan)
* Sambhar (Rajasthan)
* Wular (J & K)
* Loktak (Manipur)
* Harike (Punjab)

Based on the data collected by the Expert Group constituted by the Ministry of Environment and Forests in 1983, a directory of wetland in India was brought out by MEF in 1990. According to this inventory about 4.1 million hectares area in India is covered by wetlands. Besides, an area of about 6740 sq. km. is covered under coastal mangrove wetlands. Out of 4.1 million hectares of wetlands, 35% area has been identified as the natural wetland and the rest manmade. Statewise distribution of wetlands is presented in Table 5.

Table - 5. State/Union Territory-Wise Distribution of Wetlands in India (including wetlands of less than 100 hectares)

S.N.	State	Natural		Man-Made	
		No.	Area(ha)	No.	Area(ha)
1	Andhra Pradesh	219	1,00,457	19,020	4,25,892
2	Arunachal Pradesh	2	20,200	NA	NA
3	Assam	1394	–	–	–
4	Bihar	2	2,24,788	33	48,607
5	Goa	3	12,360	NA	NA
6	Gujarat	22	3,94,627	57	1,29,660
7	Haryana	14	2,691	4	1,079
8	Himachal Pradesh	5	702	3	19,165
9	Jammu & Kashmir	18	7,227	NA	21,880
10	Karnataka	10	3,320	22,758	5,39,195
11	Kerala	32	24,329	2,121	2,10,579
12	Madhya Pradesh	8	324	53	1,87,818
13	Maharashtra	49	21,675	1,004	2,79,025
14	Manipur	5	26,600	NA	NA

15	Meghalaya	2	NA	NA	NA
16	Nagaland	2	210	NA	NA
17	Orissa	20	1,37,022	36	1,48,454
18	Punjab	33	17,085	6	5,391
19	Rajasthan	9	14,027	85	1,00,217
20	Sikkim	42	1,101	2	3.5
21	Tamil Nadu	31	58,868	20,030	2,01,132
22	Tripura	3	575	1	4,833
23	Uttar Pradesh	125	12,832	28	2,12,470
24	West Bengal	54	2,91,963	9	52,564
	Total	2,164	14,49,338	65,250	25,87,965
	Union Territories				
1	Chandigarh	NA	NA	1	170
2	Pondicherry	3	1,533	3	1,131
	Grand Total	2,167	14,50,871	65,254	25,89,266

* Wetlands of India-A Directory 1990, Ministry of Environment and Forests, New Delhi

World Wide Fund for Nature, India, in collaboration with the Asian Wetland Bureau published a Directory of Indian Wetlands in 1993 in a format similar to the Directory of Asian Wetlands.

Under the National Mangroves Programme of MEF, 15 mangrove areas have been identified for coservation and preparation of management action plans. List of selected mangrove areas is presented in Table 6. The management plans broadly cover survey and demarcation, natural regeneration in selected areas, afforestation, protection measures (such as fencing, watch and ward facilities), and awareness programmes.

A National Strategy for the conservation of corals and coral reefs in India has been developed by the MEF. The main elements of the strategy are survey and demarcation of coral reefs; identification of problems affecting coral reefs; detailed study of flora and fauna; preparation of status report on corals in India; control of over exploitation of corals for industry through administrative notification and later, legislation; investigation of impacts of pollutants on corals; and determination of point and non-point sources of pollution; regulation of fisheries in coral reef areas; establishment of marine parks; and education and awareness programmes.

Table - 6. List of Mangroves in India Identified for Conservation and Management by the Ministry of Environment and Forests

Sr. No.	Mangrove	State
1	Koringa	Andhra Pradesh
2	Godavari delta	Andhra Pradesh
3	Krishna estuary	Andhra Pradesh
4	Coondapur	Karnataka
5	Vembanad	Kerala
6	Achra	Maharashtra
7	Ratnagiri	Maharashtra
8	Mahanadi delta	Orissa
9	Bhitarkanika	Orissa
10	Pichavaram	Tamilnadu
11	Point Calimere	Tamilnadu
12	Sunderbans	West Bengal
13	North Andaman	Andaman and Nicobar
14	Nicobar	Anadaman and Nicobar

Source : Directory of Indian Wetlands, 1993, World Wide Fund for Nature, India and Asian Wetland Bureau

4.4 WETLAND AREA LEGISLATION

Over 20 legislations regulate India's environment. Those specially relevant to wetlands include the Water (Prevention and Control of Pollution) Act, 1974, Environmental Protection Act, 1986, Water (Prevention and Control of Pollution) Cess Act, 1978, Indian Wildlife (Protection) Act, 1991 (amended), and Indian Fisheries Act, 1987.

Environmental Pollution Control legislations provide a foundation for India's basic institutional and regulatory frameworks. Under these acts, the Central Pollution Control Board (CPCB) makes policy and sets minimum national standards. The State Pollution Control Boards (SPCBs) implement these standards, and monitor and enforce to ensure compliance. These acts also prescribe a range of penalties, including both fines and imprisonment for non-compliance.

The Indian Wildlife (Protection) Act, 1972 was enacted to provide special legal protection to wildlife on a unified national basis. It contains provisions for the establishment of national parks and sanctuaries by state governments for the purpose of protecting, propagating, and developing wildlife therein, or its equivalent, and includes powers for stringent punishment if these provisions are infringed. Hunting of all animals and the destruction of flora is prohibited, except in special circumstances, when the state government can approve the granting of a permit. The complete ban on all cattle grazing and fishing in national parks indicates a higher level of protection than in wildlife sanctuaries where grazing and fishing may be either 'regulated, controlled, or prohibited'. The Act has been adopted by all the states and union territories with the exception of Jammu & Kashmir, which has a separate legislation enforced since 1978.

The Wildlife (Protection) Act was amended for the fourth time in 1991 in order to extend protection to wildlife and intensify punishment for violations. This amendment has provisions for non-governmental organisations and individuals (non-officials) to report matters of violation of the Act directly to the court after notification. Hunting of all wildlife specified in Schedules I, II, III, and IV of the 1972 Act is prohibited. These include all wetland- dependent species of birds and animals. Commercial felling and exploitation of wildlife (flora and fauna) is banned in all wildlife sanctuaries and national parks. The amended Act extends protection to plant species for the first time. Apart from the amendment to the Wildlife (Protection) Act, India has also amended its export policy in 1991, bringing a total ban on export of birds.

The protection of forests and wild animals is included in the concurrent list in the Constitution under the 42nd Amendment, 1976. This empowers Central Government to control their protective status and also to include forest areas and sanctuaries of national importance under the powers of acquisition of property. The Forest (Conservation) Act came into force in October 1980, and attempts to reduce the rate of deforestation. This controls the de-gazetting of forest lands and their improper use for commercial forestry or non-forest use. The Act supercedes the Indian Forest Act of 1927 from which the National Forest Policy of 1952 was derived.

4.5 WETLAND AREA ADMINISTRATION

The Indian Board for Wildlife (established in 1952) is the chief advisory body to the Government on matters concerning wildlife, forests, estuaries, mangroves, and general wilderness areas. It is chaired by the Prime Minister. At the state level, the 1972 Wildlife (Protection) Act established State Wildlife Advisory Boards under statutory provisions.

In 1980, the Government appointed the Tiwari Committee to recommend legislative measures and administrative machinery to ensure environmental protection. As a result of its recommendations, an independent Department of Environment was created in November 1980, and later a separate Ministry of Environment and Forest has been formed in 1985. This Ministry is responsible for planning, promotion, and coordination of all protected areas and environmental programmes in the country. The Ministry has a National Wetlands, Mangroves and Coral Reefs programme described in preceding sections. All the states (except Nagaland) have now set up their own State Departments of the Environment. At central level there is a Director, Wildlife Preservation whilst at the state level, the senior official is the Chief Wildlife Warden (replacing the former Deputy Chief Conservator of Forests). Important Sanctuaries and National Parks are generally administered by separate park and sanctuary superintendents.

CHAPTER - 5

INDICATORS FOR WETLAND ASSESSMENT

5.1 INDICATORS OF WETLAND BENEFITS

As discussed earlier benefits associated with wetalnds can be classified as functions, uses and attributes. Indicators for identification of the benefits from the wetlands during field studies are presented in Table 7.

Table - 7. Existence Indicators for Wetland Benefits and Costs

BENEFIT	EXISTENCE INDICATORS
FUNCTIONS	
Flood mitigation	Wetland • has a regulated or constricted outflow • has an outflow less than its inflow • has neither an outlet nor an inlet • does not have permanent standing water • has a high ratio of seasonally flooded area to permanently flooded area • has a permeable substrate • has a slope less than that of nearby watercourses
Prevention of intrusion of saline water	Wetland • is in low lying coastal area • has deep wells or bores which are brackish or saline much of the time is permanent

	• contributes significantly to the flow of local rivers • is tidally influenced but non-saline
Storm protection	Wetland • has a bank height greater than the mean storm water level • vegetation is rigid or deep-rooted • is in a coastal area • has many of the features • identified above as indicators of flood mitigation potential
Sediment removal	Wetland • has a regulated or constricted outflow • has an outflow less than its inflow • has erect persistent vegetation • has winding channels • has no flow or low flow velocity • has relatively long duration and large extent of seasonal flooding • has a high ratio of seasonally flooded area to permanently flooded area • has the effect of slowing the velocity of through-flowing water • intercepts overland runoff • is regularly flooded by a river • is shallow and vegetated • has a rough vegetation surface • has large numbers of filter feeders • shows direct evidence of accretion
Nutrient removal	Wetland • has a high capacity for sediment retention • has a regulated or constricted outflow • has an outflow less than its inflow • has erect persistent vegetation • has winding channels • has no flow or low flow velocity • has relatively long duration and large extent of seasonal flooding

- has a high ratio of seasonally flooded area to permanently flooded area
- has the effect of slowing the velocity of through- flowing water
- intercepts overland runoff
- is regularly flooded by a river
- is shallow and vegetated
- is permanently flooded or saturated, or tidally flooded
- has a high sediment organic content
- has high plant species diversity, with no dead forested areas

Toxicant removal

Wetland

- has a high capacity for sediment retention
- has a regulated or constricted outflow
- has an outflow less than its inflow
- has erect persistent vegetation
- has winding channels
- has no flow or low flow velocity
- has relatively long duration and large extent of seasonal flooding
- has a high ratio of seasonally flooded area to permanently flooded area
- has the effect of a slowing the velocity of through -flowing water
- intercepts overland runoff
- is regularly flooded by a river
- is shallow and vegetated

Groundwater recharge

Wetland

- has a regulated or constricted outflow
- has an outflow less than its inflow
- has a water table which slopes away from it
- has a permanent inlet but no permanent outlet
- has a permeable substrate
- is located at or below crest of a major mountain or range

	• water balance is such that infiltration rate plus inflow exceeds evapotranspiration rate plue outflow
Groundwater discharge	Wetland • has a regulated or constricted inflow • has an inflow less than its outflow • is permanently flooded • has a steeper gradient downstream of the outlet than upstream of the inlet • is stable with regard to seasonal water level fluctuations
Erosion mitigation	Wetland • has a high capacity for storm protection or flood mitigation
Nutrient export	Wetland • has a high rate of primary productivity • has a permanent outlet • is potentially eutrophic • has significant areas of erect or submerged vegetation
Wildlife habitat	Wetland • has a high plant species diversity • has a range of different vegetation structures • is relatively undisturbed • is the only one of its type in the area
Fish habitat	Wetland • has a diversity of water conditions • is relatively undisturbed
Toxicant export	Areas downstream from the wetland show signs of flora or fauna damage due to toxicants, and flora and fauna upstream do not
USES	
Forestry, agriculture, forage production	Wetland • has suitable plant species • has a high rate of plant primary productivity • shows evidence of the use
Recreation/tourism	Wetland • has a high landscape or species diversity

	• has unusual natural features • shows evidence of the use
Transport medium	Wetland • is permanently flooded or has permanent channels • shows evidence of the use
Water supply	Wetland • is permanently or at least seasonally reliably flooded • has water of an acceptable quality for human or agricultural or industrial use • is the only supply of readily obtainable water of quality and quantity acceptable to the potential users • shows evidence of the use
Mineral production	Wetland • has suitable accessible deposits • shows evidence of the use
Pest production	Wetland • contains habitat suitable for species known to be pests in the area • shows evidence of pest production
Wildlife or fish production	Wetland • contains habitat suitable for wildlife and fish species • shows evidence of this use
Aquaculture	Wetland • has a relatively stable water level • has relatively stable water quality (both physical and chemical) • has high plant primary productivity • has nutrient rich waters • shows evidence of this use
Research education site	Wetland • has high species diversity • has a range of vegetation structures • contains rare or unsusual species or species assemblages

	• shows evidence of this use
Fertilizer production	Wetland • has extractable floating plant material of acceptable nutrient content • shows evidence of this use
Energy production	Wetland • has resources such as peat or fuelwood • is tidal, with a narrow outlet and a large tidal range • is non-tidal, with a large throughflow and a constricted outlet • is elevated • shows evidence of this use
ATTRIBUTES	
Biological diversity	Wetland • has a high species diversity • is relatively undamaged • is not facing uncontrollable external threats • contains rare, threatened or endangered species • is sufficiently large to support genetically viable populations of significant species • has significant topographic, edaphic and hydrological variation
Cultural or historic value	Wetland • is included in local oral or written cultural materials • has been occupied or used over a long period • has significant cultural or historic features
Aesthetic value	Wetland • has significant natural features • has a range of landscape types • has a range of habitats • has a large number of visible or attractive species • has landscape features which are unusual in the area
Wilderness value	Wetland

- in a remote area
- is relatively uninfluenced by human activities
- is not subject to significant levels of visitation

Source : James, R.F., 1991, The Valuation of Wetlands : Approaches, Methods and Issues, PHPA/AWB, Sumatra Wetland Project Report No. 29, Boyor

5.2 INDICATORS FOR ASSESSMENT OF WETLAND ECOSYSTEM

Wetlands exhibit enormous diversity based on their genesis; geographical location; water regime; chemistry; and dominant plant, soil and sediment characteristics. The dynamics of water inflow and loss are fundamental to the development, maintenance and functioning of wetlands. Inflow-outflow balance is influenced primarily by climate and catchment configuration while the storage is controlled by local geomorphology and geological characteristics.

Table - 8. Wetland Indicators

Category	Indicator
Physical Indicators	Size of wetland Shape of wetland Water depth Water quality Topography Location of inflow/outflow points Geomorphology Geology Climate
Biological Indicators	Species diversity Species composition Primary productivity
Biophysical processes	Sediment balance Nutrient balance Toxicant removal
Socio-economic Indicators	Cultural/aesthetics importance Population dependent on wetland products

Wetland hydrology in turn influences the physical and chemical characteristics of the wetlands which have major implications for both flora and fauna, as well as for ecosystem dynamics.

Indicators for assessing the health of wetland ecosystems can be categorised as :

- Hydrological Indicators
- Biological/Ecological/Limnological Indicators
- Physico-chemical Indicators

Table - 9. Biological Indicator Species in Wetlands

S.N.	Wetland Type	Indicator Species
1	Peat Swamp Forest	*Gonystylus bancanus* *Palaquium burckii* *Palaquium microphyllum* *Durio carinatus* *Campnosperma auriculata* *Shorea spp.*
2	Non-Peat Swamp Forest	*Alstonia pneumatophora* *Campnosperma spp.* *Shorea spp.* *Nauclea spp.* *Syzygium spp.* *Diospyros spp.* *Garcinia spp.* *Melaleuca spp.*
3	Mangroves	*Rhizophora apiculata* *Rhizophora mucronata* *Bruguiera gymnorrhiza* *Bruguiera cylindrica* *Bruguiera parviflora* *Bruguiera sexangula* *Ceriops tagal* *Kandelia candel* *Sonneratia alba* *Sonneratia caseolaris / acida* *Sonneratia ovata* *Avicennia alba* *Avicennia marina* *Avicennia officianalis* *Xylocarpus granatum* *Xylocarpus moluccensis*

A list of indicators for assessing the health of wetlands is presented in Table 8. Biological indicator species in select wetland types are presented in Table 9.

CHAPTER - 6

ENVIRONMENTAL IMPACT ASSESSMENT

6.1 CONCEPT OF EIA

Environmental impact assessment is potentially one of the most valuable, inter-disciplinary, and objective decision-making tools with respect to alternate routes for development, process technologies and project sites. It is an ideal anticipatory mechanism allowing measures that ensure environmental compatibility in our quest for socio-economic development.

There is no universally accepted definition of EIA. Some commonly used definitions are:

- EIA consists in establishing quantitative values for selected parameters which indicate the quality of the environment before, during, and after the action (Heer and Hagerty, 1977).
- EIA is an assessment of all relevant environmental and resulting social effects which would result from a project (Battelle, 1978).
- EIA is an activity designed to identify and predict the impact on the biogeophysical environment and on man's health and well-being of legislative proposals, policies, programmes, projects and operational procedures, and to interpret and communicate information about impacts (Munn, 1979).
- EIA is a process to identify, predict and to describe in appropriate terms the prosandcons (benefits and penalties) of a proposed development. To be useful, the assessment needs to be communicated in terms understandable by the community and decision-makers and the pros and cons should be identified

on the basis of criteria relevant to the countries affected (UNEP, 1980).

– EIA is the systematic examination of environmental consequences of projects, policies, plans and programmes. Its main aim is to provide decision-makers with an account of implications of alternative courses of action before a decision is made (Clark, 1984).

– EIA is a formal study process used to predict the environmental consequences of the proposed developmental project, find ways to reduce unacceptable impacts, and shape the project so that it suits the local environment, and present these predictions and options to decision-makers (UNEP, 1988).

EIA is a process that has the objective of providing decision makers with an indication of the likely consequences of their actions. This is achieved through impact identification, prediction, evaluation and mitigation stages which endeavour to answer the questions:

* what will changes in environmental quality due to proposed developmental activity?
* what will be the extent of the changes?
* do the changes matter? and
* what can be done about them?

Over the years, it has become increasingly clear that the environmental clearance of the project proposals by the competent authority is not the sole decision point in EIA. Decision making starts much earlier, may be at the stage of selection of site, raw materials and production process, and extends to feedback mechanisms in the form of environmental monitoring during the operation phase.

EIA is no longer seen as an add-on process. The greatest contribution of EIA to environmental management is in reducing adverse impacts by devising measures beyond those warranted by emission standards and environmental management regulations. It is now generally accepted throughout the world that the benefits of project level EIA considerably outweigh its costs. In recent years, the outcome of EIA studies ranges from simple impact statements to changes in project sites, manufacturing processes, raw materials, engineering designs, introduction of additional pollution control measures, landscaping, manpower training programmes, compensation for restoration of damaged resources, and off-site programs to enhance quality of life in the community likely to be affected due to proposed developmental activity.

6.2 EVOLUTION OF EIA WORLDWIDE

United States of America was the first country to assign mandatory status to EIA vide its National Environmental Protection Act (NEPA) of 1969. A host of industrialized countries have since implemented EIA procedures. Canada, Australia, the Netherlands and Japan adopted EIA legislation in 1973, 1974, 1981 and 1984 respectively. In July 1985 the European Community (EC) issued a directive making environmental assessments mandatory for certain categories of projects (Wood, 1994).

Among the developing countries, Columbia was the first Latin American Country to institute a system of EIA in 1974. In Asia and Pacific region, Thailand and Philippines have long-established procedures for EIA. EIA was made mandatory in Sri Lanka in 1984. A manual for EIA was prepared and published in 1988 in Sri Lanka (NBRO, 1988). There is dearth of information on the general situation in Africa, although a number of nations including Rwanda, Botswana and Sudan have experience of EIA (Wathern, 1988).

Bilateral and Multilateral agencies have also recognised the value of EIA as a decision-making tool. The Organization for Economic Co- Operation and Development (OECD) issued recommendations on EIA in its constituents states in 1974 and 1979, and for development aid projects in 1986. OECD issued guidelines for good practices in EIA in 1992 (OECD, 1992). United Nations Environment Programme (UNEP) in 1980 provided guidance on EIA of the development proposals (UNEP, 1980) and supported research on EIA in developing countries (Ahmad and Swamy, 1985). UNEP, in 1987 vide the decision 14/25 of the Governing Council, set out goals and principles of EIA for the member countries (UNEP, 1987) and provided guidance on basic procedures for EIA in 1988 (UNEP, 1988).

The World Conservation Strategy pinpointed the need to integrate environmental considerations with development in 1980 (IUCN, 1980). EIA has become an integral part of World Bank policy (1987), which states that environmental issues must be addressed as part of overall economic policy. In 1989, the World Bank issued the Operational Directive on Environmental Assessment (O.D. 4.00) which was revised and updated in October 1991 (O.D. 4.01). Asian Development Bank in 1990 published guidelines for EIA (ADB, 1990). Importance of EIA was echoed in the Brundtland Report (WCED, 1987), and at the Earth Summit on environment and development at Rio de Janerio in 1992 (UNCED, 1992).

As foreseen by Garner and O'Riodan (1982) development of EIA, as a tool for decision making world-over, has emerged through following stages :

* No formal accounting; decisions made on interest group lobbying and engineering feasibility; primary emphasis on economic development
* Conventional cost-benefit analysis; emphasis on efficiency criterion and engineering feasibility; major concern still economic development
* Innovative cost-benefit analysis, use of multiple objectives and discount rates, imaginative proxy pricing mechanisms; economic development as one of the objectives
* EIA mainly concerned with describing the repercussions of the proposals on bio-physical processes; economic development still primary objective
* EIA with more attention given to socio-cultural as well as bio-physical systems, economic development principle but not the sole objective
* EIA at two tier level, first to look at generic issues associated with the large projects as a class, second to investigate how an "approved" scheme can best be designed with minimal net social and bio-physical disruption. EIA visualized as a creative participatory environmental management activity.

The summary of evolution of EIA in various countries is presented in Table - 10 (Kulkarni, 1995).

Table - 10. Evolution of EIA in Various Countries

Country	Basis of Implementation
Australia	Environmental Protection (Impact of Proposals) Act 1974, Commonwealth of Australia
California	California Environmental Quality Act (CEQA) of 1971
Canada	Federal Environmental Assessment and Review Process Guidelines Order 1984, Canada
China	Environmental Protection Law, 1979
France	Law on Protection de la Nature, 1978
India	Notifications dated May 5, 1994 under the Environment Protection Act, 1986
Japan	Principles for Implementing EIA by Environmental Agency, 1984
New Zealand	Resource Management Act 1991, New Zealand
Sri Lanka	National Environmental Act 1980, amended in 1986

Thailand	Improvement and Conservation of National Environmental Quality Act 1975, amended in 1978
The Netherlands	EIA Policy, 1986
United States	US National Environmental Policy Act of 1969
United Kingdom	Environmental Assessment Guidelines, 1989
Western Australia	Environmental Protection Act 1986, Western Australia
West Germany	Cabinet resolution, September 1975

Source : Kulkarni, V.S., (1995) Development of Methodology for Computer Aided EIA of Industrial Projects, Thesis submitted for Doctor of Philosophy to Nagpur University, India

6.3 EVOLUTION OF EIA IN INDIA

Environmental Impact Assessment (EIA) of developmental projects was first introduced in India in 1977-78 when Planning Commission advised the then Department of Science and Technology to take up environmental appraisal of river valley projects. Subsequently, projects in mining, industry, thermal power, nuclear power, port and harbour sectors were brought under the purview of EIA. At present, the Ministry of Environment and Forests (MEF) is the nodal agency for EIA in India.

The MEF published guidelines for preparation of EIA statements along with questionnaires and checklists for industrial projects (MEF, 1985). Project proponents are required to provide relevant information as indicated in the guidelines alongwith the Environmental Impact Assessment Statement/Environmental Management Plan (EMP). A preliminary scrutiny of the project proposals is made by the technical experts of MEF. After ensuring that the main aspects are covered, EIA reports are placed before the Appraisal Committees of Experts. The Appraisal Committee discusses the impact of the project with the project proponents and, if necessary, site visits are made for on-the-spot assessment of various environmental aspects. Based on their examination, the Appraisal Committees make recommendations on approval or rejection of the proposal by MEF. The environmental clearance to development projects is subject to implementation of stipulated safeguards under the provisions of Environment (Protection) Act 1986, Forest (Conservation) Act 1980, and other rules and regulations in force.

The MEF on January 27, 1993, brought out a draft notification under the Environment (Protection) Act 1986 making environmental clearance mandatory for expansion or modernization of any activity if pollution load is to exceed existing levels, and also for new projects listed in schedule - I of the notification. The notification was subsequently modified in May 1994 (MEF, 1994).

Over the years 1989-94, 1286 EIA reports have been appraised at MEF (Kulkarni, 1995).

6.4 HIERARCHY IN EIA

The EIA studies could be categorized as site selection studies, rapid/ comprehensive/regional EIAs, and carrying capacity studies.

Site selection studies involve evaluation of the alternative sites with respect to environmental and project attributes such as proximity to raw materials, infrastructural facilities, markets etc. The study aims at ranking of site alternatives for objective decision making.

Rapid EIA differs from Comprehensive EIA with respect to timeframe for baseline data collection. Rapid EIA refers to assessment based on one season (3 months) monitoring whereas Comprehensive EIA relates to assessment based on three seasons (9 months) monitoring for baseline data. Rapid EIA facilitates decision-making in those situations where a fair amount of knowledge exists about the proposed site or the impacts of the proposed development. Rapid EIA also helps in identifying significant issues for comprehensive EIA.

Regional EIA relates to development in/of a region based on three season data collection and addresses itself to the analysis of assimilative capacity of air, water and land components of environment. The scope of carrying capacity study is extended to the analysis of supportive capacity in the region with respect to resource availability/utilization, supply/demand, infrastructure/ congestion, and assimilative capacity/residuals.

6.5 MAJOR ISSUES IN EIA

EIA has been regarded as both science and art, reflecting the concern related to technical aspects of appraisal and the effects of EIA upon the decision making process. Further, decisions are often shaped rather than made or taken. Everyone involved in policy formulation, planning and impact assessment studies as well as in public hearings, reviews, legislative/media debates is in fact playing a part in shaping decisions (Munn, 1979).

The design of an effective EIA methodology can be envisaged as the search for mechanisms to deal with issues generated by the need to juxtapose the planning and environmental clearance of project proposals. Some issues deal with technical matters such as impact

Project Requiring Environmental Clearance as per Schedule-I, MOEF Notification

1 Nuclear power and related projects such as Heavy Water Plants, nuclear fired complex rare earths

2 River valley projects including hydel power major irrigation and their continuation including food control

3 Ports, barbous airports except minor ports and harbours

4 Petroleum refineries including cride and product pipelines

5 Chemical Fertilizers (Nitrogenous and Phosphatic) other than single superphosphate

6 Pesticides (Technical)

7 Petrochemical complexes (both Olefinic and Aromatic) and Petro-chemical intermediates such as DMT, Caprotactom LAB etc. and production of basic plastic such as 11 PDE, HPDE, PPPVC

8 Bulk drugs and pharmaceuticals

9 Exploration for oil nad gas and their production, tranporation and storage

10 Synthetic rubber

11 Asbestos and asbestos products

12 Hydrocyamic acid and its derivatives

13 Primary metallurgical industries (such as production of iron and steel, aluminium copper zinc, lead and ferro alloys) Electric are furnaces (minor steel plants)

14 Chlor alkali industry

15 Integrated paint complex including manufacture of resins and basic raw materials required in the manufacture of paints

16 Viscose staple fibre and filament yarn

17 Storage batteries intogreated with manufacture of oxides of lead and lead antimony alloy

18 All tourism projects between 200 m - 500 m of high water line and at locations with an elevation of more than 1000 m with investment of more than Rs. 5 crores

19 Thermal power plants

20 Mining projects (with lease more than 5 hecatres)

21 Highway projects

22 Tarred roads in Himalayas and or Forest area

23 Distilleries

24 Raw skins and hides

25 Pulp, paper and newsprint

26 Dyes

27 Cement

28 Foundries (individual)

29 Electroplaning

identification and prediction while others relate to the management of information. The major issues in EIA process are:

* Identification of projects requiring EIA
* Identification of impacts to be assessed
* Assessment of impacts
* Completion of an appraisal
* Enabling the objectivity in appraisal

From the technical point of view, EIA can be considered as a data management process. It has three components. First, the appropriate information necessary for a particular decision to be taken must be identified and, possibly, collected. Secondly, changes in environmental parameters resulting from the implementation of the project must be determined and compared with the situation likely to accrue without the project. Finally, actual change must be recorded and analysed.

6.6 CLASSIFICATION OF ENVIRONMENTAL IMPACTS

The term 'impact' and 'effect' are frequently used synonymously in EIA literature, although some researchers have advocated differentiating between natural and man-induced changes, in the biogeophysical environment, effects, from the consequences of these changes, i.e. impacts (Munn, 1979). An impact has both spatial and temporal components and can be described as the change in an environmental parameter over a specified period and within a defined area resulting from a particular activity compared with the situation which would have occurred had the activity not been undertaken.

Impacts can be classified as (Rau and Wooten, 1980):

* adverse or beneficial
* caused or induced
* primary/secondary/tertiary
* short term/long term
* reversible/irreversible
* site specific/project specific

Impacts can also be classified as :

* Socio-economic impacts
* Biological and physical impacts
* Cultural impacts

6.7 PROJECT SCREENING

EIA procedure needs be appplied only to those actions which lead to significant environmental consequences. It is important to establish mechanisms for the selection of actions requiring EIA. Screening allows elimination from the review process of all those projects that do not require detailed EIA, thus avoiding unnecessary expense and delays in project clearance.

Screening methods are based on :

- project thresholds
- positive and negative lists
- matrices
- initial environmental examinations

Projects thresholds method relies upon the establishment of threshold values for key features of the project or its environment. If a threshold is exceeded then EIA is required.

Reliance upon one threshold may give rise to an incorrect decision. It is, therefore, a normal practice to link a series of different thresholds together. Thresholds, while being simple, may need frequent revision particularly in the light of experience, and inflation when financial criteria are used.

Positive lists are compiled through a review of existing developments, identifying those projects that give rise to significant environmental damage. Lists are one of the simplest approaches to screening. The preparation of lists involves one major problem, viz. individual projects of the same general type or class may have considerable variations in size of plant, process and layout which may give rise to varying environmental consequences. In addition, gaining the acceptance of all parties on the entry of individual project types on particular lists (mandatory positive, intermediate and negative) may be difficult and time consuming.

Project screening criteria, based on thresholds and lists, advocated by various countries/agencies are summarised in Table 11 (Kulkarni, 1995).

The United Nations Environmental Programme (UNEP, 1980) as also the Asian Development Bank (ADB, 1990) have developed questionnaires for the assessment of industrial activities, termed as Initial Environmental Examination (IEE), which provide a simplified decision tool for screening of projects for EIA. Guidelines for site screening are also published by UNEP (1980).

Table 11. Select Screening Criteria for Industrial Projects

I. Thailand

Petrochemical	:	Raw material requirement 100 TPD or more
Oil refining	:	All
Natural gas	:	All
Chlor-alkali	:	production capacity 100 TPD or more
Iron and steel	:	Production capacity 100 TPD or more
Cement	:	All
Smelting	:	Smelting capacity 50 TPD or more
Wood pulp	:	Production capacity 50 TPD or more

II. The Philippines

- Non-ferrous metal industries
- Iron and steel mills
- Petroleum and motor-chemical industries including oil and gas
- Smelting plants
- Power plants

III. Sweden

- Iron and metal works
- Large saw mills
- Factories producing organic and inorganic chemicals
- Plants processing nuclear fuels
- Oil refineries
- Fossil fuel power plants exceeding 500 MW
- Fertilizer
- Cement

IV. Commission of European Communities

Projects to be subjected to mandatory EIA

- Crude oil refineries (excluding undertakings manufacturing only lubricants from crude oil) and installations for gasification and liquification (greater than 500 tonnes or more of coal or bituminous shale per day)
- Thermal power stations and other combustion installations (with a heat output of 300 MW or more)
- Integrated works for the initial melting of cast-iron and steel

- Installations for the extraction, processing and transformation of asbestos and products containing asbestos (installations for asbestos-cement products - annual production greater than 20,000 tonnes of finished product, for friction materials - greater than 50 tonnes of finished product per annum, and for other uses of asbestos - more than 200 tonnes per annum)
- Integrated chemical installations

Projects to be subjected to EIA when appropriate (Member State to decide on case to case basis)

- Glass
- Chemical
- Food processing
- Textile
- Leather
- Pulp and paper
- Rubber

V. OECD (1986)

- Chemical plants
- Power plants
- Industrial processes generating toxic wastes
- Pulp mills

VI. The World Bank

Category A : projects which affect the environment significantly through direct pollutant discharges that are large enough to cause degradation of air, water or soil; large scale physical distaurbances of the site and/or surroundings; extraction, consumption, or conversion of substantial amounts of forest and other natural resources; hazardous materials in more than incidental quantities; and involuntary displacement of people and other significant social disturbances. Large industrial plants and plants involving manufacture, transportation, and use of pesticides and other hazardous and/or toxic materials are included in Category A projects. These projects require full environmental assessment.

Category B : projects often differ from Category A projects of the same type only in scale. These projects require limited environmental assessment.

Category C : projects do not require environmental assessment.

The final decision on classification of project rests with the Task Manager.

Source : Kulkarni, V.S., (1995) Development of Methodology for Computer Aided EIA of Industrial Projects, Thesis submitted for Doctor of Philosophy to Nagpur University, India

Notwithstanding the fact that EIA of industrial projects in carried out in India since 1984, no explicit screening criteria were available in India till 1994. The projects appraised by the MEF included (MEF, 1993):

- Projects which require approval of the Public Investment Board/Planning Commission/Central Electricity authority
- Projects referred to MEF by other Ministries
- Projects which are sensitive and located in environmentally degraded areas
- Projects of Public sector undertakings of the Government of India where the project cost is more than Rs. 20 crores

The MEF, vide its notification of May 1994, has made environmental clearance mandatory for expansion or modernization of any activity if pollution load exceed existing levels, and also for new projects listed in Schedule-I of the notification.

6.8 SITE SELECTION CRITERIA

The magnitude of environmental impacts of projects is, in most of the cases, site specific. Hence, the selection of site should form an integral part of EIA. The World Bank has advised its Task Managers to specifically consider project locations in the categorisation of the projects for further environmental assessment (World Bank, 1991).

In India, the Ministry of Environment and Forests (MEF, 1985) stipulated that the industrial sites should maintain the following distances from the areas listed below:

* Ecologically and/or otherwise sensitive areas : at least 25 kms, the requisite distance may be increased depending on the geo- climatic conditions
* Coastal areas: at least 1/2 km from high tide line
* Flood plains of the riverine systems : at least 1/2 km from flood plain or modified flood plain affected by dam in the upstream or by flood control systems
* Transport/communication systems: at least 1/2 km from highways and railways
* Major settlements (more than 3,00,000 population) : distance from settlements is difficult to maintain because of urban sprawl. At the time of siting of the industry if any notified limit of any major settlement is within 50 km, the spatial direction of growth of the

settlement for at least a decade must be assessed and the industry shall be sited at least 25 km from the projected growth boundary of the settlement.

The list of ecologically or otherwise sensitive areas drawn by the MEF is presented in Table 12.

Table - 12. List of Ecologically and/or Otherwise Sensitive Areas

1	Religious and historic places
2	Archaeological monuments/ sites
3	Scenic areas
4	Hill resorts
5	Beach resorts
6	Health resorts
7	Coastal areas rich in corals, mangroves, breeding grounds of specific species
8	Estuaries rich in mangroves, breeding grounds of specific species
9	Gulf areas
10	Biosphere reserves
11	National parks and sanctuaries
12	Natural lakes, swamps
13	Seismic zones
14	Tribal settlements
15	Areas of scientific and geological interests
16	Defense installations, specially those of security importance and sensitive to pollution
17	Border areas (international)
18	Airports

The MEF has further stipulated that the following factors must be recognized in siting:

* No forest land shall be converted into non-forest activity for the industry (Forest Conservation Act, 1980)
* No prime agricultural land shall be converted into industrial site
* Within the acquired land the industry must locate itself at the lowest location to remain obscured from general sight
* Land acquired should be sufficiently large to provide space for appropriate treatment of wastewater after maximum possible in-house recycle and reuse. Reclaimed (treated) wastewater shall be used for raising green belt and, if possible, for aquaculture

* The green belt between two adjoining large scale industries shall be one kilometer
* Enough space shall be provided for storage of solid wastes
* Layout and form of the industry must conform to the landscape of the area without affecting the scenic features at that location
* Associated township of the industry must be created at a space having phytographic barrier between the industry and the township.

Ideally, the site for an industrial project should be selected based on the regional carrying capacity (Khanna *et al.*, 1991) which is defined as the maximum rate of resource consumption and waste discharge that can be sustained indefinitely in a defined planning region without progressively impairing bio-productivity and ecological integrity.

6.9 EIA METHODOLOGIES

The identification and assessment of environmental impacts of developmental activities are complex because of the diversity of impacts caused by human interference to the environmental and social systems. Impact identification and assessment requires collection and collation of large amount of diverse data and, most importantly, communicating the final results to the decision makers and members of the public, many of whom are unlikely to be experts in environmental science. It is precisely to help overcome these difficulties that most EIA methods have been devised.

The need for systemization and interdisciplinary studies in EIA led to the development of common structured framework for relating different kind of data. Also, the task of comparing alternative project sites for industries demanded an assessment which allowes direct comparisons to be made between the alternatives. The variety of structured approaches to EIA developed to fulfill these tasks are generally known as EIA methodologies or methods.

Although there is a large number of EIA methodologies which have been developed and used in EIA, the variety is more apparent than real. Nearly all methods are variants of general types which have specific organizing principles in common. These are checklists, matrices, networks, overlays and models. In case of checklists and matrices there are many versions whereas there are fewer examples of networks and models available. All these methodologies are generic in nature and are adapted to specific type of project assessment such as industrial, water resources, mininig, etc.

CHAPTER - 7

EIA FOR PROTECTION OF WETLANDS

7.1 IMPACTS OF DEVELOPMENTAL ACTIVITIES ON WETLANDS

Wetlands are seriously affected due to pressures from rapid urbanisation, agriculture, aquaculture and industrial development; increasing levels of pollution; over-exploitation; and hydrological alterations.

Due to lack of adequate public awareness, wetlands are considered to be wastelands providing habitats for breeding and growth of mosquitoes and molluscs which serve as vectors of a number of diseases like malaria, filariasis and schistosomiasis. Malaria epidemics caused by Anopheles mosquitoes have been, and continue to be, major cause of human suffering and mortality in the Indian subcontinent. Large areas of seasonal wetlands are therefore considered undesirable by urban planners. In traditional landuse planning, wetlands are drained and filled with soil (also used for solid waste disposal). Wetlands are then used for urban settlements, industrial development and agriculture.

In coastal areas intertidal areas are generally chosen for aquaculture to take advantage of natural tidal flushing. The rapidly proliferating shrimp culture activity in the recent past is also responsible for the destruction of coastal wetlands in India.

Wetlands are also significantly affected due to construction of dykes, dams, levees and seawalls for flood control, water supply, irrigation and stream protection which upset the free movement of water and ecological balance.

Mining of wetland soils for peat, coal, gravel, phosphate and other materials, and ground water abstraction are responsible for the clearing of wetland vegetation and reduction in biological diversity.

Heavy urban and industrial development in coastal zones causes an influx of pollutants into coastal and esturine areas. A significant amount of pesticides, herbicides and nutrients are carried in agricultural run-offs and sediments. Wetland food chain is essentially detritus based food chain which is affected due to influx of toxicants, leading to reduction in the productivity of wetlands.

As a result of eutrophication processes due to discharge of wastewater, agricultural run-off and other man made causes such as mining, erosion etc., the wetlands are increasingly invaded by noxious growth of a number of exotic and native weed species, e.g. *Salvinia, Eichhornia, Typha, Pistia, Hydrilla* etc.

Impact of developmental activites on the wetlands are summarised in Tables 13 and 14.

Table - 13. Developmental Activities that affect Wetlands

Project Activities	Primary Impact
Change in drainage pattern Channelization of rivers Diversion of flow Construction of dam Extraction of ground/surface water	Change in hydrological regime
Development of township Development of road network Industrial activity	Change in drainage pattern
Removal of vegetation from catchment Harvest of wetland products Afforestation Introduction of alien floral species	Alteration of floral composition
Harvesting of fauna Introduction of alien fauna	Alteration of faunal composition
Removal of nutrients Addition of nutrients Compaction Earthworks	Alteration of substrate
Discharge of domestic / industrial wastewater	Pollution

7.2 STEPS IN EIA

7.2.1 Impact Identification

Impact identification involves :

* Identification of project activites that could affect the wetlands
* Identification of wetlands in the impact zone of the project
* Identification of benefits associated with each of the wetlands in the project area
* Identification of wetlands benefits likely to be affected due to proposed project

The methodology for impact identification proposed herein employs questionnaire checklist for identification of project activities, and matrix for identification of wetland benefits. Worksheets for impact identification have been presented in Worksheets 1,2 and 3.

The project information for identifying environmentally relevant project activites normally documented in the project feasibility reports. Information on the existence of wetlands near the proposed project site could be obtained from the Directory of Wetalnds prepared by MEF and also by WWF. Information can also be obtained from topographic maps, vegetation surveys, and soil surveys available with various institutions. In absence of secondary data, field survey would be required.

7.2.2 Scoping of Studies

Scoping involves identification of significant impacts for further investigations. This could be achieved through exclusion of those benefits which do not occur from the wetlands at the site or have little or no importance.

The potential benefits can be assessed based on existence and importance indicators delineated in Table - 7. Using these indicators important benefits should be listed for further investigation.

7.2.3 Field Data Collection

The objective of field data collection is to establish status of the wetlands which may get affected due to the proposed developmental activities and provide basis, if possible, for impact quantification/ assessment.

Issues to be considered in EIA

* Impact on soil, water (hydrological regime, ground water and surface water)
* Impact on land use, forest, agriculture, fisheries, tourism, recreation etc.
* Socio-economic impact including short and long term impact on population
* Impact on Health
* Impact on flora and fauna (wildlife) particularly on endemic and endangered species
* Cost benefit analysis including the measures for environmental protection
* Safeguards and control measures proposed to prevent or mitigate the adverse environmental impacts
* Plants for rehabilitation of project oustees
* Contingency plants for dealing with accidents/disasters
* Monitoring and feed back mechanism on implementation of necessary safeguard (e.g. setting up of Environmental Management Cells)

Field data collection activities would involve :

* Collection of data for wetland indicators delineated in Table - 8
* Collection of data on landuse, vegetation cover, biological diversity in the terrestrial ecosystem as also socio-economic status of the population directly/indirectly dependent on the wetland benefits

7.2.4 Impact Prediction

Prediction of impacts on the wetland benefits due to proposed developmental activity involves projecting the existing environmental setting into the future, with and without the project, and then performing necessary calculations for predicting real impacts of the proposed development. Quantitative impact prediction requires the greatest degree of scientific application.

Table 14. Impact of Project Activities on Wetland Benefits

Potential Benefits	Primary Impact					
	Alteration of hydrological regime	Induced development	Alteranation of floral composition	Alternational of faunal composition	Alteration of substrate	Pollutant discharge
Functions						
Flood mitigation	*	*	*		*	
Prevention of intrusion of saline waters	*	*	*		*	
Storm protection	*	*	*	*	*	*
Sediment removal	*	*	*		*	*
Nutrient removal	*	*	*		*	*
Toxicant removal	*	*	*		*	*
Groundwater recharge	*	*	*			*
Groundwater discharge	*	*	*			*
Erosion mitigation		*	*	*	*	*
Nutrient export	*	*	*		*	*
Wildlife habitat	*	*	*	*	*	*
Fish habitat	*	*	*	*	*	*
Toxicant export	*	*	*		*	*
Uses						
Forestry	*	*	*		*	*
Agriculture	*	*	*		*	*

Forage production	*	*	*	*	*	*
Recreation/tourism	*		*		*	
Transport medium	*		*		*	*
Water supply	*	*	*			*
Mineral production	*	*	*		*	*
Pest production	*	*	*	*	*	*
Wildlife production	*	*	*	*	*	*
Fish production	*	*	*	*	*	*
Aquaculture	*	*	*	*	*	*
Research site	*	*	*	*	*	*
Education site	*	*	*	*	*	*
Fertilizer production	*	*	*	*	*	*
Energy production	*	*	*		*	
Attributes						
Biological diversity	*	*	*	*	*	*
Cultural or historic value	*	*	*	*	*	*
Aesthetics value	*	*	*	*	*	*
Wilderness value	*	*	*	*	*	*

Impact prediction enables understanding of:

* Magnitude of impact (severity)
* Extent of impact (areal coverage)
* Duration of impact (temporal coverage)

Traditionally wetlands have been used for the disposal of domestic and industrial wastewaters. This results in undesirable impacts on aquatic flora and fauna. The majority of these changes are brought about by the discharge of organic matter (BOD) resulting in lowering in the concentration of dissolved oxygen (DO) in the receiving water. Pollution of wetlands is also caused by the discharge of toxic substances, which may break down due to chemical or bacterial action (non-conservative) or may be resistent to breakdown (conservative). Other problems arise due to discharge of inorganic nutrients causing excessive algal growth. In all these situations it is important to be able to relate the rate of discharge of pollutant to resulting concentrations in the receiving water.

An important application of mathematical modelling is to obtain a continuous profile of water quality out of observed sparse data. Once the continuous profile is obtained, it is possible to relocate or rationalize the water quality monitoring networks. Continuous profile of water quality could also be obtained for different conditions where response of water quality system could be extrapolated (simulation). Surface water quality models have been used over several decades to determine waste treatment levels and effluent standards so that the receiving streams would meet the water quality criteria for their best designated usages.

The assumptions pertaining to the mixing of pollutants in wetlands dictate the spacial dimensionality of the model. Although all real physical systems are three-dimensional, sufficient accuracy may be obtained in many river systems by modelling only one or two dimensions. One-dimensional models assume complete mixing in the vertical and lateral directions. Two dimensional models may assume either uniform lateral mixing, as in stratified estuaries, or vertical mixing as in relatively shallow and wide rivers.

Most of the water quality models in actual use today are extensions of two fairly simple equations proposed by Streeter and Phelps in 1920s. Often used with these BOD-DO models are other first-order exponential decay, dilution, and sedimentation models for conservative and non- conservative substances. Relatively recently complex multi- parameter water quality models have been proposed and applied to predict more accurately the physical, chemical, and biological interactions of many constituents and organisms found in natural water bodies. These multi-constituent water quality simulation models generally require more data and computer time but they also provide detailed and comprehensive information on the quantity and quality of water resulting from various water and land management policies.

In the past two decades there has been an increasing emphasis on the effects of various constituents, specially nutrients, on the aquatic ecosystem, i.e. on the production of phytoplankton, zooplankton, fish and other trophic levels within the natural water bodies.

Mathematical models are available for prediction of impact of wastewater discharges on water quality of rivers, lakes and estuaries. Software packages available in public domain from US EPA for prediction of impact on water quality include QUAL2-E for streams and WASP for lakes and estuaries.

The complexity and variability of biological and socio-economic systems make precise quantitative predictions of impact of developmental activities impossible. Hence, impact on biological and socio-economic environment is quantified in terms of appropriate indicators.

The assessment of potential environmental impacts warrants selection of a reference point from which biotic and abiotic changes can be measured. The reference point is usually an intact ecosystem which is compared with its affected or stressed counter-part. Indicators employed for terrestrial and aquatic ecosystem assessment alongwith the measurement techniques are summarised in Tables 15 and 16, respectively.

Table 15. Indicators of Biological Environment : Aquatic Ecosystem

Parameter	Analysis Method	Significance of Parameters
Species Diversity (Zooplankton)	Sedgewick Method Shannon Weaver Index d $d - \left[\frac{ni}{n}\right] \log2 (ni/n)$ ni = number of individuals of each individual species in a sample n = total number of individuals of all species in the sample	Species diversity shows the health of an ecosystem. Low species diversity is an indication of eutrophic stage.
Species diversity (Phytoplankton)	Calculation V = t x d x W x L V = volume of the sample 'observed' (mm3) t = number of observed transects d = depth of the cell cavity (mm) W = width of the microscope field (mm) L = length of the cell cavity (mm)	Like zooplankton

	Organism = n(V/u) 1/C x 1000 where, n = total no.of individuals in observed transacts V = volume of the sample in counting cell (mm) u = volume of observed transects (mm) Original volume of sample (ml) C = concentration factor = Volume of sample conc. (ml) Results = express as organism/L	
Similarity & Pielou Indices (Zooplankton & Phytoplankton)	$\text{Similarity Index} = \frac{2C}{A+B}$ A = no. of species in x sampling station B = no. of species in y sampling station C = no. of species in common to both sampl. stations $\text{Pielou Index} = E = \frac{d}{\log 2\ S}$ d = Shannon Wiever Index S= number of Species in the community	1. Similarity index analyses similarity between two aquatic ecosystems 2. Pielou Index helps in identifying stresses on ecosystem by comparing species available in ecosystem & polluted ecosystem
Benthic fauna (microzoobenthos)	Sieve analysis to collect micro and macro inverberates. Chemical analysis to float benthic fauna on the surface. Count the number of individuals of each species	
Commercial fisheries	Fish catch/ha/Year - fish catch/ha/Year for different species of fishes from lotic & lentic habitat - average value of fish/tonnes - no.of fisherman involved	Shows the productivity of fish & its demand in the market Analyses the harvest potential (low, high, very high)
Rare and Endangered Species	List of fish available at lotic & lantic habitat is collected The list is then compared with the Rare & Endangered species list for following five categories: Rare/Threatened/ endangered/endemic/extinct	Proper protection may be given to those species which are rare & endangered. Identified list may help to take decision whether these plants need special attention for growth & development.

Source : Kulkarni, V.S. (1995)

The impact on socio-economic environment can be assessed in terms of Quality of Life (QOL). Differnt agencies have employed indices to measure quality of life (QOL) in terms of economic, social, physical, health and ambient environmental quality issues. These indices mainly vary in terms of parameteric selection for computation of QOL. A summary of parameters considered in various computations of QOL is presented in Table 17.

Table - 16. Indicators of Biological Environment : Terrestrial Ecosystem

Parameter	Analysis Method	Significance of Parameters
Dominance, Census and Similarity Indices	Dominance Index = Count of most dominant species/total count Census Index = no.of individuals of each species recorded/no.of kilometers covered Similarity Index = 2C/(A+B) where, A = no.of species in A station B = no.of species in B station C = no.of species common to A and B	Dominance index indicates distribution of various species Similarity index compares two sampling locations
Pest species	Weigheted distribution of pest species	Helps to identify the expected impact on the productivity of any cropland. The cropland can be managed properly based on the information available on pest species
Rare and Endangered Animal/ Birds Species	Classification of rare and endangered animal and bird species	Proper protection may be given to rare and endangered animal and bird species if such species occurs in study area. Identified list may help in taking decision if these species require special attention for growth & development
Browsers & Grazers	Nos. per hectare	This parameter help to analyse carrying capacity of a grassland. If browsers & grazers are more in the grassland then the grassland can not support them so it may browse on agriculture field or encroach nearby forests. This parameter helps to identify the status of browsers & grazers in the ecosystem
Terrestrial Natural Vegetation	$\text{Density} = \frac{\text{No. of species A}}{\text{Area sampled}}$ Relative Density = $\frac{\text{Density of species A}}{\text{total density of all species}} \times 100$	To determine the density and relative densities of a particular species

Terrestrial Natural Vegetation	Frequency = $\frac{\text{No. of plots in which species A occurs}}{\text{Total no. of plots sampled}}$ Relative Frequency = $\frac{\text{Frequency value for species A}}{\text{total of frequency values for all species}} \times 100$	To determine frequency and relative frequency of a particular species in sample plots
Terrestrial Natural Vegetation	Dominance = $\frac{\text{total cover V basal area of species A}}{\text{area sampled}}$ Relative dominance = $\frac{\text{dominance for species A}}{\text{total dominance for all species}} \times 100$	To determine dominance and relative dominance of a species in sample plots
Terrestrial Natural Vegetation	Importance value = (Relative density + relative dominance + relative frequency)/3	Importance value index is the indication of importance of different species. The species having lowest importance value has to be preserved and protected. Proper maintenance is required to protect those species having low importance value. If proper protection is not given to those species they may also become endangered in near future
Rare and Endangered Plant Species	List of species available in the study area to be collected from Forest Department & may be compared with Red Data Book for Indian Plants Prepare list of species under following categories: - rare; - threatened; - endangered - exlinct; - endemic	The list give rare and endangered plant species available in the area
Pest Species (Plant)	Weighted distribution of pest species present in the area	If density, frequency, & abundance of pest species are more, then their immediate eradicated is necessary since these species may affect the normal growth & development of the ecosystem
Crop Productivity	Productivity = $\frac{\text{Crop produced kgs}}{\text{Area hectares}}$	This shows the status of agroecosystems & its productivity
Cropping Pattern	Percent area under different crops	This shows the types of crops grown in that area

Source : Kulkarni, V.S., (1995)

According to USEPA, QOL is defined as a function between objective conditions and subjective attitudes involving a defined area of concern (EPA, 1974). The computation of quality of life involves following steps :

* Computation of objective QOL index

$$QOL_o = \sum_{i-1}^{m} QI_i \times W$$

QOL_o = Objective QOL index

QI_i = Objective Quality Index for i^{th} factor

W = Weight of the ith factor

m = Number of factors

* Computation of subjective QOL index

$$QOL_s = 1/P \sum_{j-1}^{P} \sum_{i-1}^{m} QI_{ij} \times W$$

QOL_s = Subjective QOL index

QI_s = Subjective Quality Index (VFC) for i^{th} factor

W = Weight of the ith factor

m = Number of factors

P = Sample Population Size

* Computation of aggregate QOL index

$$QOL = \frac{QOL_o + QOL_s}{2}$$

The description of select parameters that could be used in computation of objective QOL is presented in Table 18.

7.2.5 Impact Evaluation

Impact evaluation involves assessing the status of wetland ecosystem as also benefits of wetlands with and without the proposed developmental activity. Impact evaluation provides useful information on how the proposed developmental activity will affect the wetlands.

Wetlands sometimes provide benefits which can contribute to the success of a project (e.g. water supply, shoreline protection and erosion control). In many cases projects affect benefits which are of value to communities, natural processes or other projects. Impact evaluation enables assessment of the extent and cost of the management plan required to mitigate adverse impacts due to developmental activities.

Table - 17. Summary of Select QOL Indices

Developer	Factor List
PA	• economic environment
	• political environment
	• social environment
	• physical environment
	• health
	• natural environment
Perloff	• work places
	• community neighbourhood
	• household shelter
	• transportation utilities
	• natural environment
	• spatial environment
Moss	• welfare benefits
	• general government
	• regulation and safety
	• recreation and culture
	• national defence
	• human resource development
	• housing environment and utilities
	• space
Gross and Springer	• income and group values
	• urban conditions
	• crime & delinquency
	• natural environment
Wilson	• individual status
	• economic growth
	• welfare
	• individual equality
	• state & local government
	• professionalism

Flax	• education • technological change • living conditions • health • agriculture • income • unemployment • poverty • racial equality • community concern • citizen participation • public order • educational attainment • social disintegration • housing • transportation • health • mental health • air quality

Source : EPA (1974)

Table 18. Parameters used in computation of objective quality of life factors

Major Factors	Objective Indicators
1. Economic Environment	
Income	Per capita disposable income Median family income
Income Distribution	Gini coefficient of income distribution
Economic Security	Income support Wealth measures
Work Satisfaction	Accident, productivity, and turnover rates
2. Social Sector	
Family	Marriage and divorce rates Illegitimate births
Community	Social responsibility scale

Social Stability	Upward social mobility Social disorder incident rates
Physical Security	Violent crime rates
Culture	Human effort directed toward the arts
Recreation	Persons participating in outdoor recreation and average days per person
3. Political Environment	
Electoral participation	Per cent of registrants voting
Non-electoral participation	Bloomberg & Rosenstock's "Action Score"
Government Responsibility	Budget allocations Per capita distribution of funds
Civil Liberties	Rights Commission Citizen review board
Informed Constituency	Content analysis of mass media
4. Health	
Physical	Infant mortality tate Physicians/capita Health care facility utilization
Mental	Persons in mental hospitals/population Per cent of patients "cured"
Nourishment	Per capita consumption of food types Nutrients consumed per day per capita
5. Physical Environment	
Housing	Per cent deteriorated houses Per cent lacking plumbing Per cent overcrowded
Transportation	Family costs Per cent budget allocated to construction and maintenance
Public Services	Cost of gas and electricity Frequency and coverage of services
Material quality (both goods and services)	Product life Automobile recalls Cost and frequency of repairs
Aesthetics	Litter, billboards Trees preserved and planted
6. Natural Environment	
Air Quality	People exposed to sub-standard conditions Concentration of CO, NO2, SO2

Water Quality	BOD, Coliform count, Turbidity, temperature, pH
Radiation	Amount of radioactivity in water, soil, body burden
Toxicity	Lead concentrations Cases of lead poisoning
Solid Wastes	Kg/capita Amount recycled Frequency of collection
Noise	Community noise

Source : EPA (1974)

A large number of options are available for impact evaluation. These options include simple checklists, scaling, weighing checklists, matrices and cost benefit analysis.

Use of checklist for impact evaluation involves assessing impact on wetland indicators and benefits using a scheme to describe impact as highly adverse to highly beneficial as illustrated in Table - 19.

Condensing information on complex environmental variables into some manageable form is a recurrent problem in assessment. Scaling weighing checklists have been devised to enable all adverse/ beneficial impacts for a single project, or more usefully, alternative projects to be compared in the form of quantitative indices. Available are quasi-mathematical methods in which impacts are weighted in terms of relative importance, transformed into units from a common, notional scale and finally manipulated mathematically to form impact indices. The most well-known of these methods is the Battele Environmental Evaluation System (BEES) employed for water resources projects by Dee et al. (1973).

This method is essentially concerned with the determination of environmental quality of an area without a project, and then predicting a net positive or negative change, should the project be implemented. This involves predicting the future state of the environment without the project in the same time-scale as that used to predict the project-affected environment. The major feature of BEES is that environmental impacts are expressed in commensurate units providing common units for comparison. The steps involved in the development of commensurate units include transformation of parameter estimates into an environmental quality (EQ) scale, assignment of importance units to the individual parameters (PIU), and the multiplication of

Parameters Establishing Quality of Life in Indian Condition

Parameter	Measurements
Housing	Housetype, number of rooms, family size, expenditure on housing/month, satisfaction level about housing
Education	Number of literates in the family, satisfaction level about education facility
Employment and working conditions	Number of family members employed, job satisfaction level, working conditions, satisfaction level about wages and perks
Income	Family income from all sources, per capital income, satisfaction level about income
Clothing	Expenditure for clothing for family per year, average number of dresses purchased per family member, satisfaction about clothing
Nutrition	Main food, supplementary food, quantity of milk used per day, quantity of vegetables used per day, expenditure on food per month, satisfaction with health facilities.
Health	Number of vehicles in the family, expenditure on transportation per month, satisfaction with public transport facilities
Transporation	Most common ailment in family, expenditure on health per month, type of medical facility availed, satisfaction with the health status, satisfaction with health facilities.
Community	Satisfaction with communication facilities, availability of personal telephone.
Energy	Cooking fuel, quanity of fuel used per month, expenditure on cooking fuel per month, satisfaction with fuel availability, electricity bill per month, satisfaction with electricity supply
Water Supply and Sanitation	Source of supply, satisfaction with water supply (quality and quantity), satisfaction with sanitation facilities, satisfaction with drainage facilities
Environment and Pollution	Major pollutants, ambient air and water quality, satisfaction with physical environment of the area, satisfaction with social environment, satisfaction with aesthetics environment.
Recreation	Availability of radio/TV/VCR/news paper at home, frequency of visiting recreation centres, expenditure on recreation per month, satisfaction with recreation facilities.
Social Security	Type of saving, amont saved per month, satisfaction with police protection.

Source : NEERI (1995), Carrying Capacity Based Development Planning of Doon Valley, Report submitted by National Environmental Engineering Research Institute, Nagpur to Ministry of Environment and Forests, New Delhi.

scale values by importance values to obtain environmental impact units (EIU). Typical outcome of impact evaluation using BEES is presented in Table 20.

Table 19. Checklist for Impact Assessment

Potential Benefits	Impact on Wetland Benefit : Enter as HA/SA/NI/SB/HB					
	Wetland No. 1	Wetland No. 2	Wetland No. 3	Wetland No. 4	.....	....
Functions						
Flood mitigation						
Prevention of intrusion of saline waters						
Strom protection						
Sediment removal						
Nutrient removal						
Toxicant removal						
Ground water recharge						
Groundwater discahrge						
Erosion mitigation						
Nutrient export						
Wildlife habitat						
Fish habitat						
Toxicant export						
Uses						
Forestry						
Agriculture						
Forage production						
Recreation/tourism						
Transport medium						
Water supply						
Mineral production						
Functions						
Pest production						
Wildlife production						
Fish production						
Aquaculture						
Research site						

Education site						
Fertilizer production						
Energy production						
Attributes						
Biological diversity						
Cultural or historic value						
Aesthetics value						
Wilderness value						

Legend: HA - Highly Adverse; SA - Slightly Adverse; NI- No Impact SB - Slightly Beneficial; HB - Highly Beneficial

Table 20. Impact Evaluation Using Battelle Environmental Evaluation System

Parameter	Maximum score	Alternatives		
		No Project	With project	With project and Impact Mitigation Plan
Ecology				
Forests	205	115	95	105
Crops	240	175	150	165
Environmental Pollution				
Land Degradation	130	90	70	80
Noise Levels	70	60	50	55
Aethetics				
Topography	40	30	26	27
Landuse	65	50	40	45
Traffic conjestion	50	40	35	38
Human Interest				
Employment	50	10	20	25
Economic Benefit	100	30	70	80
Safety compared to rail/road	50	50	40	45
Total	1000	650	596	665

Source: NEERI (1994), Environmental Impact Assessment of Proposed Crude Oil Pipeline for BORL Refinery in Madhya Pradesh, Report submitted by National Environmental Engineering Research Institute to Bharat Oman Refineries

Difficulties with scaling weighing checklists relate to the derivation of weights and focus on parameters which can be quantified to the extent that there is a great temptation to quantify the unquantifiable, eg. aesthetics. Many subjective elements are subsumed within both the weighing scheme and the value functions. In effect, the basis for decision is created by the method. The preferred option and, hence, the only decision that logically can be taken is one with the highest score for environmental quality.

BEES is complex to operate and any Environmental Impact Statement (EIS) prepared using this or a similar method would not be comprehended easily by non-experts. Not only would the technical information on impacts needs to be understood, but also the principles of the method need to be comprehended. Finally, the complexity of this approach results in requirements of large manpower, time and resource requirements.

Matrix methods are two-dimensional checklists in which possible project activities are established along one axis, with potentially impacted environmental characteristics or conditions along the other. Thus the cause-effect relationships between specific activities and impacts are identified in matrix methods.

Matrix is useful to present the results of an appraisal. This could be achieved by characterising impacts in terms of magnitude and importance on a common 1-10 scale, where 1 is least magnitude or importance, and 10 the greatest. The magnitude of an impact is taken to be an expression of its scale, e.g. the geographical area of the impact. The score for importance may, however, be different. Importance refers to the significance of the impact. If a visual impact were to occur in an area of poor landscape quality then a score of only 2 or 3 may be awarded instead of 8 or 9 in an area of high quality.

The scores for magnitude and importance should be included in the appropriate cell of the matrix representing a likely impact. The cell should be bisected by a diagonal line with the score for magnitude being placed in the top left-hand corner. The score for importance is placed in the bottom right-hand corner. These scores can be accompanied by a plus sign (+) to indicate a beneficial effect. A completed matrix would consist of a number of cells containing two numerical scores and, in some cases, a plus sign. Use of matrix in impact evaluation is illustrated in Table 21.

The cost-Benefit analysis method of impact evaluation involves evaluation of environmental impacts in monetary units to facilitate easy comparison with other costs and benefits of the project.

The use of CBA warrants working of environmental personnel alongside economists and engineers throughout the entire planning

Table 21. Matrix for Impact Assessment of Project Activities on Wetland Benefitis

Potential Benefits	Primary Impact					
	Alteration of hydrological regime	Induced development	Alteration of floral composition	Alteration of faunal composition	Alteration of substrate	Pollutant discharge
Functions						
Flood mitigation						
Prevention of intrusion of saline waters						
Storm protection						
Sediment removal						
Nutrient removal						
Toxicant removal						
Groundwater recharge						
Groundwater discharge						
Erosion mitigation						
Nutrient export						
Wildlife habitat						
Fish habitat						
Toxicant export						
Uses						
Forestry						

Agriculture						
Forage production						
Recreation/tourism						
Transport medium						
Water supply						
Mineral production						
Pest production						
Wildlife production						
Fish production						
Aquaculture						
Research site						
Education site						
Fertilizer production						
Energy production						
Attributes						
Biological diversity						
Cultural or historic value						
Aesthetics value						
Wilderness value						

process. Duplication of efforts is thus eliminated and costs of feasibility studies reduced. Most importantly, the decision maker, when reviewing the project, would not view environmental considerations as separate or auxiliary to economic development. Although developing countries may be far from putting this approach into practice, it is a goal to work towards for those concerned with balancing environment and development. Various options for assessment of wetland costs and benefits are presented in Table 22.

Table 22. Techniques for Valuation of Wetland Benefits and Costs

Benefit or Cost Type	Valuation Techniques
Direct Use	Net Social Benefit
	Market Price Methods
	– Market Price – Shadow price
	Surrogate prices
	–Substitute price – Cost of relocation – Indirect substitute price – Value in trade – Indirect opportunity cost
	Value in Production
	– Production function approach – Net factor income
	Travel Cost
Indirect Use	Protection of Assets
	– Cost of replacement – Rehabilitation cost – Value of lost production – Additional establishment cost – Cost of relocation
	Hedonic Pricing
	Value in Production
	– Production function approach – Net factor income
	Surrogate Prices
	– Substitute price – Indirect substitute price
	Contingent Valuation
Preservation Value	Contingent Valuation

Source : James, R.F., (1991)

Criteria for Selection of EIA Methodology

* Comprehensive with respect to intricate systems of living and nonliving element bound together by complex interrelationship in environment.
* Flexibility with respect to size and scale of impacts caused by different projects
* Detection of short and long term true impacts resulting from a project (compared to the impact that would occur at no proejct option)
* Objectivity for providing impersonal unbiased and respectable measurement immune to tampering by political and other external forces
* Asssurance with respect of necessary expertise for sound, experienced and professional judgment
* Utilization of maximum and appropriate state-of-art to draw on best available analytical techniques.
* Employment of explicity defined evaluation criteria
* Assessment of actual magnitude of impacts based on specific levels of impact for each environmental concern
* Provision for overall assessment for total project by aggregating multiple individual impacts
* Pinpoining of critical impacts in terms of intensity, magnitude or hazardous nature of impact.

7.2.6 Impact Mitigation

Mitigation measures are interventions which reduce, avoid or offset potentially adverse consequences of developmental projects (Khadka, 1995). A wide range of mitigation measures may be proposed to prevent, reduce or compensate for each advesre impact assessed as significant. Mitigation measures include :

* Changing project sites, routes, engineering design, processes, raw materials, fuels, operational methods, disposal routes or locations, and safety requirements
* Measures for ecological restoration such as landuse planning, conservation programmes planning and reforestation schemes

* Introducing pollution control devices, or resource recovery based waste treatment methods
* Offering restoration of damaged resources, compensation to affected persons, initiation of programmes to enhance environmental quality and consequently the quality of community life
* Environmental education before, during and after the implementation of developmental project

Implementation of mitigation measures requires funding, which should be estimated and included in the EIA report. All proposed measures should be integrated in project design so that these measures may automatically form part of the construction and operational phases of the project.

7.2.7 Post Project Monitoring

EIA is a continuing activity which should be integrated with the operational phase of the project through formulation of Post Project Monitoring (PPM) Programme. PPM could be used to ascertain whether the conditions imposed on the project proponent, such as specific mitigation measure, have been effectively implemented. In the long term it may allow unexpected impacts to be remedied or relaxation of conditions discovered to be unnecessarily stringent.

PPM involves actual measurement of impacts on various environmental components vis-a-vis EIA predictions. In addition, it involves routine monitoring of influents and effluents from the wetlands. PPM should specify locations of monitoring stations, parameters, and frequency of sampling; sample collection and analysis methodology; and technique for statistical analysis of data.

7.2.8 Public Participation in EIA

Attempts towards wetland conservation and management have little chance of success without local community participation. In fact, much loss of wetlands in the past has occurred because local people have been ignored in the process of development through the imposition of National priorities over local needs, which often alienates and impoverishes impacted communities.

Consultation with, and involvement of, local communities in all stages of management planning through survey, project design, implementation, monitoring and evaluation, is absolutely necessary. For this process to be effective, local communities must have sufficient awareness of the rationale behind the project to make their participation meaningful. There is no doubt that in the past negative or unacceptable facets of development projects have been withheld from locals in the hope that their judgements on the project would err on the positive side. Consultation and awareness building needs to be carried out before the project is being designed. Only then will local people have an adequate grasp of what the project is trying to achieve and how it will affect them. Only then can they help make truly informed decisions.

It is generally agreed that local people know how to manage their resources. Also, local population is the main beneficiary group which is likely to be adversely affected by the developmental projects. Public participation is thus required at the time of scoping of EIA studies as also for finalization of draft EIA report. This process is important in order to underastand both the nature and extent of socio-economic impacts and acceptibility of mitigation measures, particularly to the affected groups.

Various forums for eliciting public participation in the EIA process are :

* Scoping sessions including public meetings
* Studies/surveys of affected people
* Public meetings and workshops for fine tuning of mitigation options
* Microplanning/ participatory appraisal

Methodologologies for eliciting views of affected people are :

Direct Methods

* Public meetings
* Discussions with specialists (Non-Government)
* Meetings with people's representatives
* Meetings with NGOs
* Attitudinal surveys

Indirect Methods

* Hire field researchers working at site
* Meetings with NGOs representing sub-grous
* Questionnaire surveys

Pre-requisites for effective public participation are :

* Preparation of communication material comprising :
  - Technical information presented in verńalcular
  - Audio-visual aids that can be made available to diverse population
  - Us of Digrams/graphics/pictures
* Dissemination of information as pamphlets, media reports etc.
* Appropriate settings for public meetings could be created through:
  - Putting people at ease by location and physical surroundings of meeting
  - Expressing respect to people in the proceedings
  - Use of local language

Tools for Public Participation

Purpose	Tools
Educational/Information	Newspaper articles, radio and TV programs, speeches and presentations, field trips, exhibits, information depositories, school programs, films, brouchers and newsletters, reports, letters, conferences
Review/Reaction	Briefings, public meetings, public hearings, surveys and questionnaires, question and answer columns, advertised "hotlines" for telephone inquiries
Interaction Dailogue	Workshops, special task forces, interviews, advisory boards, informal contacts, study group discussions, seminars.

Public awareness building and participation in project planning and implementation should form an integral part of EIA for wetland protection. The effectiveness of EIA is determined by how sucessfully the communities have been involved in the process.

Indegenous people generally have an historical relationship with their lands and a holistic traditional scientific knowledge of natural resources and environment. Their participation in National and International sustainable development decisions should be strengthened.

A process to empower indegenous communities should recognize their values, traditional knowledge and resource management practices, and their dependence on renewable resources and ecosystems. Their lands should be protected from environmentally unsound activities and from activities indegenous people consider to be socially and culturally inappropriate.

Source : Agenda - 21, Chapter 26, United Nations Conference on Environment and Development, Rio de Janerio, 3-14 June, 1992.

Environmental Impact Assessment, as a National instrument, should be undertaken for proposed activities that are likely to have significant adverse impact on the environment and are subject to a decision of a competent national authority"; EIA is poised to play a significant role in planning for sustainable development.

Source : Rio Declaration - Principle 17

REFERENCES

ADB, (1990), Environmental Guidelines for Selected Industrial and Power Development Projects, Office of the Environment, Asian Development Bank, Bangkok.

Battele Institute, (1978), The Selection of Projects for EIA, Commission of the Europian Communities Environment and Consumer Protection Service, Brussels.

Bisset, R., (1984), Selected EIA Methods : An Introduction, Paper presented at the International Training Coures on Environmental Impact Assessment and Land-use Planning, Hong-kong, 16-21 January.

Clark, B. D., (1984), Environmental Impact Assessment : Scope and Objectives in Perspectives in Environmental Impact Assessment, D. Reidel Publishing Company, Holland.

Commission of Europian Communities, (1985), On the Assessment of Effects of Certain Public and Private Projects on the Environment, Official Journal, L175, 28.5.85.

Cowardian, L.M., Carter, V., Golet, F.C. and LaRoc, E.T. (1979). Classification of wetlands and deep water habitats of the United States, US Fish and WL Serv., Washington D.C.

Dee, N., Baker, J.K., Drobny, N.L., Duke, K.M., Whitman, I. and Fahringer, D.C., (1973), An Environmental Evaluation System for Water Resources Planning, Water Resources Research, Vol. 9, No. 3, pp. 523-535.

EPA, (1974), Studies in Environment - Vol. II - Quality of Life, EPA-600/5-73-012b, Office of Reserach and Development US Environmental Protection Agency, Washinton D.C.

Go, F.C., (1990), Environmental Impact Assessment, MARC report no. 41, Monitoring Assessment Research Centre, London.

Heer, J. E. and Hagerty, D. J., (1977), Environmental Assessment and Statements, Van Nostrand Reinhold, New York.

Htun, N., (1988), The EIA Process in Asia and Pacific Region in P. Wathern ed. Environmental Impact Assessment : Theory and Practice, UNwin Hyman, London.

IUCN (1971). The Ramser Conference : Final Act of the International Conference on the Conservation of Wetlands and Water Fowl. Spl. Supply IUCN Bull., 2(19):1-4.

Howe, C.P., Claridge, G.F., Hughes, R., and Zuwendra, (1991), Manual of Guidelines for Scoping EIA in Tropical Wetlands, PHPA/ AWB Sumatra Wetland Project Report No. 5, Asiam Wetland Bureau-Indonesia and Directorate General for Forest Protection and Nature Conservation, Department of Forestry, Bogor.

IUCN, (1980), World Conservation Strategy - Living Resources Conservation for Sustainable Development, International Union for Conservation of Nature and Natural Resources, Gland, Switzerland.

James, R. F., (1991), The Valuation of Wetlands : Approaches, Methods and Issues, PHPA/AWB, Sumatra Wetland Project Report No. 29, Bogor.

Khanna, P., Kulkarni, V.S., Joshi, V., Dutt, P.S., Agarwal, A.L., (1991), Carrying Capacity Based Developmental Planning Process, Journal of Indian Association of Environmental Management, Vol. 18, No. 1&2, pp. 12-19.

Kulkarni, V. S., (1995) Development of Methodology for Computer Aided EIA of Industrial Projects, Thesis submitted for Degree of Doctor of Philosophy to Nagpur University.

Kulkarni, V.S., S.N. Kaul and R.K. Trivedy, (2001). A Handbook of Environment Impact Assessment, Scientific Publishers (India), Jodhpur. (In press).

MEF, (1985) Environmental Guidelines for Siting of Industrial Projects, Ministry of Environment and Forests, Government of India.

MEF, (1994), Environmental Impact Assessment Notification : 1994 (as amended on 4.5.1994), Ministry of Environment and Forests, Government of India.

Munn, R.E., (1979), Environmental Impact Assessment : Principles of Procedures, International Council of Scientific Unions, Scientific Committee on Problems of Environment, Report-5 (SCOPE-5).

NBRO, (1988), Environmental Assessment Procedure for Development Activities in Urban Areas : A Manual for Planners and Decision Makers, National Building Research Organization, Ministry of Local Government Housing and Construction, Sri Lanka.

Odum, E.P. (1971). Fundamentals of Ecology, Saunders College Publishing, New York.

Odum, E.P. (1983). Basic Ecology, Saunders College Publishing, New York.

OECD, (1986), Recommendations of the Council on Measures required to Facilitate the Environmental Assessment of Development Assistance Projects and Programmes, C(86)26, Organization for Economic Co-operation and Development, Paris.

OECD Development Assistance Committee, (1992), Guidelines on Environment and Aid : Good Practices for Environmental Impact Assessment of Developmental projects, Development Co-operation Directorate, Paris.

Rau, J.G., and Wotten, D.C., (1980), Environmental Impact Analysis Hand Book, Mc Graw-Hill, New York.

Streeter, H. W. and Phelps, E. B., (1925), A Study of the Pollution and Natural Purification of the Ohio River, Bulletin of the US Public Health Service.

Tomlinson, P., (1984), Project Screening Methods paper presented in International seminar on Environmental Impact Assessment, University of Aberdeen.

UNCED, (1992), Rio Declaration, United Nations Conference on Environment and Development Rio de Junerio.

UNEP, (1980), Environmental Assessment Statement - A Test Model Presentation, UNEP Regional office and UN Asian and Pacific Development Institute, Bangkok.

UNEP, (1980), Guidelines for Assessing Indutrial Environmental Impact and Environmental Criteria for Siting of Industry, UNEP Industry and Environmental Guidelines Series, Vol. 1, UNEP Industry and Environment Office, Paris.

UNEP, (1988), Environmental Impact Assessment : Basic Procedures for Developing Countries, United Nations Environment Programme, Nairobi.

USAID, (1980), Environmental Design Considerations for Rural Development Projects, US Agency for International Development, Washington D.C.

Wathern, P., (1988), Introduction in Wathern, P. (ed) Environmental Impact Assessment : Theory and Practice, Unwin Hyman, London.

Wathern, P., (1988), The EIA Directive of the Europian Community in P. Wathern ed., Environmental Impact Assessment : Theory and Practice, Unwin Hymann, London.

WCED, (1987), Our Common Future, World Commission on Environment and Development Oxford University Press, London.

Whitman, I.L., (1971), Design of Environmental Evaluation System, Battelle Columbus Laboratories, Columbus, Ohio.

Wood, C., (1994), The Environmental Assessment of Plans Programmes and Policies : A Comparative Review, Indo-British Workshop on Environmental Impact and Risk Assessment of Petrochemical Industry and Environmental Audit, January 8-10, 1994, Nagpur, India.

World Bank, (1987), Environment, Growth and Development, Development Committee Paper 14, The World Bank, Washington D.C.

World Bank, (1989), Operational Directive 4.00, Environmental Assessment, The World Bank, Washington, D.C.

World Bank, (1991), Operational Directive 4.01, Environmental Assessment, The World Bank, Washington, D.C.

Worksheet No. 1

Identification of Wetlands in the Study Area

Sr. No.	Type	Locations
1	Peat Swamp Forest	
2	Other Swamp Forest	
3	Non-Forested Swamp – Overflow Wetlands	
4	Non-Forested Swamp – Other Wetlands	
5	Mangroves	
6	Coral	
7	Seagrass and Seaweed	
8	Lakes	
9	Estuaries	
10	Rivers	
11	Tidally Irrigated Rice Fields	
12	Rainfed Rice Fields	
13	Non-Rainfed Rice Fields	
14	Fishponds/Aquaculture	
15	Salt Pans	
16	Unclassified	

Worksheet No. 2

Identification of Project Activites Likely to Affect Wetlands

Sr. No.	Activity	Part of Project?
1	Change in drainage pattern	Yes/No
2	Channelization of rivers	Yes/No
3	Diversion of flow	Yes/No
4	Construction of dam	Yes/No
5	Extraction of ground/surface water	Yes/No
6	Development of township	Yes/No
7	Development of road network	Yes/No
8	Industrial activity	Yes/No
9	Removal of vegetation from catchment	Yes/No
10	Harvest of wetland products	Yes/No
11	Afforestation Introduction of alien floral species	Yes/No
12	Harvesting of fauna Introduction of alien fauna	Yes/No
13	Removal of nutrients Addition of nutrients	Yes/No
14	Compaction Earthworks	Yes/No
15	Discharge of domestic / industrial wastewater	Yes/No

Worksheet No. 3

Identification of Potential Benefits of Wetlands

Potential Benefits	Wetland Location					
	1	2	3	4	.....	.....
Functions						
Flood mitigation						
Prevention of intrusion of saline waters						
Storm protection						
Sedimental removal						
Nutrient removal						
Toxicant removal						
Groundwater recharge						
Erosion mitigation						
Nutrient export						
Wildlife habitat						
Fish habitat						
Toxicant export						
Uses						
Forestry						
Agriculture						
Forage production						
Recreation/tourism						
Transport medium						
Water supply						
Mineral production						
Pest production						
Functions						
Wildlife production						
Fish production						
Aquaculture						
Research site						
Education site						
Fertilizer production						
Energy production						
Attributes						
Biological diversity						
Cultural or historic value						
Aesthetics value						
Wilderness value						

Worksheet - 4

Data on Wetland Indicators*

Wetland Location:

Category	Indicator
Physical Indicators	Size of wetland
	Shape of wetland
	Water depth
	Water quality
	Topography
	Location of inflow/outflow points
	Geomorphology
	Geology
	Climate
Biological Indicators	Species diversity
	Species composition
	Primary productivity
Biophysical process	Sediment balance
	Nutrient balance
	Toxicant removal
Socio-economic Indicators	Cultural/aesthetics importance
	Population dependent on wetland products

* to be prepared in text form for each wetland

Worksheet No. 5

Matrix for Impact Assessment of Project Activities on Wetland Benefits

Wetland Location :

Potential Benefits	Primary Impact					
	Alteration of hydrological regime	Induced development	Alternation of floral composition	Alteration of faunal composition	Alteration of substrate	Pollutant discharge
Functions						
Flood mitigation						
Prevention of intrusion of saline waters						
Storm protection						
Sedimental removal						
Nutrient removal						
Toxicant removal						
Groundwater recharge						
Erosion mitigation						
Nutrient export						
Wildlife habitat						
Fish habitat						
Toxicant export						
Uses						
Forestry						
Agriculture						
Forage production						
Recreation/tourism						
Transport medium						
Water supply						
Mineral production						

Pest production						
Wildlife production						
Fish production						
Aquaculture						
Research site						
Education site						
Fertilizer production						
Energy production						
Attributes						
Biological diversity						
Cultural or historic value						
Aesthetics value						
Wilderness value						

Note : In each cell enter magnitude (M) and importance (i) of the primary impact on wetland benefit on scale 1-10 where 1 is least magnitude or importance and 10 the greatest

Worksheet No. 6

Cost of Mitigation

Sr. No.	Benefit Affected due to Project	Proposed Mitigation Option	Agency Responsible for Implementation	Cost of Implementation

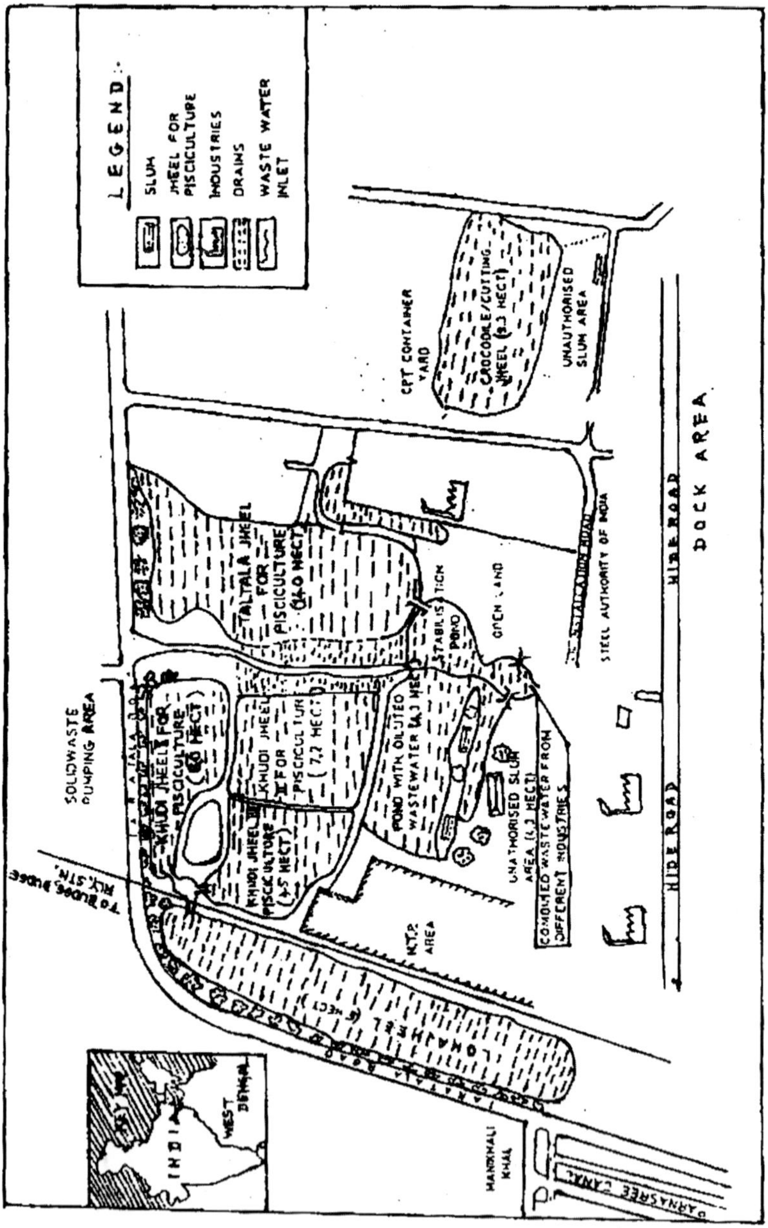

Fig. 1. Sketch Plan of Jheels in CPT Area

CASE STUDY 1

EIA OF INDUSTRIAL AND MUNICIPAL WASTEWATER DISCHARGES ON WETLANDS IN CALCUTTA PORT TRUST AREA

National Environmental Engineering Research Institute

Nagpur 440 020

1. OBJECTIVE

Indiscriminate discharge of industrial and municipal wastewater into jheels (marshy wetlands) in CPT area has severely affected the wetland ecosystem. Impact of wastewater discharges has been quantified to assess present status of wetland ecosystem so as to design environmental management plan for improvement of water quality and ecosystem productivity.

2. PROJECT SETTING

The site of the project is in the Calcutta Port Trust (CPT) area. CPT has a large wetland on the western part of its leased out property which has 48 hectares of wetlands (jheels) that receive wastewater from the adjoining 152 industries and domestic establishments (Table 1). Distribution of wetlands (jheels) is presented in Table 2 and Figure 1.

Raw waste water is fed to the wetlands at the north-eastern end of the Taltala jheel through multiple inlets. After successively passing through Khudi-I, Khudi-II and Loha jheels, the wastewater is discharged into Manikhali canal which eventually joins the river Hoogly. Crocodile jheel, on the other, is a single compartment water body receiving wastewater at the north-eastern end while the effluent from the jheel is disposed off in the river Hoogly through the Netaji Subhash Dock.

Table 1. Wastewater Sources Contributing to the Wetlands

Sl. N.	Type of Industries	No. of Industries	Wastewater Flow (m3/day) (Approx)
1	Engineering Industries	65	1728.6
2	Chemical Industries	26	15489.6
3	Godowns/Garages	42	1505.6
4	Institution	4	2015.6
5	Miscellaneous Industries	15	1050.6
	Total	152	21790.0

Table 2. Summary of Wetland Distribution

Sr. N.	Wetland	Area (Hectares)
1	Crocodile Jheel	9.3
2	Taltala Jheel	14.0
3	Khudi-I Jheel	8.0
4	Khudi-II & III Jheel	11.7
5	Loha Jheel	5.0
	Total	48.0

3. IMPACT IDENTIFICATION

Major impacts of industrial and domestic wastewater discharges on the wetland ecosystem were identified using checklist and results are presented in Table 3.

Table 3. Impact Identification

Indicator	Impact
Hydrological	
Flowrate	***
Flowrate distribution	**
Water surface elevations	**
Marsh surface elevations	**
Flood-frequency and intensity	*
Physico-chemical	
pH	***

Temperature	**
DO	***
BOD	***
Suspended solids	***
Nitrogen	***
Phosphorus	***
Chlorides	***
Pesticides	***
Heavy metals	***
Biological/Ecological	
Autecological	
Density of species	
Frequency of species	
Indicator species	
Population	
Regenerative capacity	
Community	
Growth form and structure	
Seral stage in succession	
Diversity index	
Importance value index	
Limnology	
Ecological pyramid	
Food chain	
Primary productivity	
Biomagnification	

Legend : ***: Significant impact; **: Slight impact; *: No impact

4. BASELINE DATA COLLECTION

Sampling and analysis for establishing baseline status of the wetland was carried out in 1990-1992. Summary of baseline data collection for wetland hydrology, water quality and ecosystem are presented in Tables 4 throgh 11. Performance of the wetlands in terms of removal of organic matter and pathogens was also investigated in the study (Table 12).

Table 5. Baseline Data : Physico-Chemical Water Quality

Parameters	Raw sewage	Crocodile Jheel		Taltala Jheel		Khudi-I Jheel		Khudi-II Jheel		Loha Jheel	
		Influent	Effluent	Influent	Effluent	Influent	Effluent	Influent	Effluent	Influent	Effluent
Temperature (°C)	28-29.5	29-29.5	29.5-30	27-29	27-28	–	26.5-27	–	26-27.1	–	26-27
pH	5-6.7	7-7.1	7.1-7.5	7.2-9.3	7.3-8.3	7.5-8.0	7.5-9.0	–	7.5-8.6	7.2-8.6	7.2-8.6
Alkalinity ($CaCO_3$)	424-430	435-440	364-380	180-240	172-240	–	204-302	–	176-294	170-250	164-232
Chlorides(Cl)	359-380	340-357	324-380	226-276	226-301	–	280-286	–	261-281	250-270	221-259
Total Solids	1046-1084	1156-1120	932-1088	844-1018	930-1018	–	850-982	–	682-982	–	736-898
Suspended Solids	62-82	38-40	7-70	116-156	116-164	–	80-204	–	76-146	–	53-108
Dissolved Solids	984-1062	1118-1120	895-1023	862-728	728-862	–	774-778	–	752-778	–	629-790
Total Volatile Solids	238-302	220-222	124-202	170-280	170-289	–	204-266	–	198-270	–	176-330
Dissolved Oxygen (OD)	1.5-1.7	1.7-2.7	3.2-10	5.6-7.5	8.6-12.7	–	10-12.9	–	9.8-10.8	8.5-8.9	8.7-9.5
BOD	30-70	140-142	11-27.4	28-33.5	21-33.5	–	21.5-28	–	16-26.5	15-25.2	10-24.5
COD	74-208	373-375	30-67	119-171	97-161	–	59-126	–	29.7-120	–	29.5-89
Ammonia (N)	6-7	4.2-5.9	3.2-5.7	bdl-1.8	0.5-1.8	–	0.5-2.8	–	0.5-2.8	–	1-2.3
Nitrate (N)	94.-9.6	3-8.2	0.30-7.5	0.95-1.2	0.7-1.4	–	0.7-6.5	–	0.7-5.8	–	0.7-3.98
Total Nitrogen (N)	61.0-62.5	30.8-31	33.5-33.8	18.2-31	31-31.5	–	15-18	–	13.2-15	–	7.5-10.5
Phosphate (P)	0.0850-0.86	0.53-0.55	0.03-1.60	0.4-5.30	0.13-4	–	0.30-0.82	–	0.29-036	–	0.15-13.2
Sodium (NA)	230-240	240-275	245-280	230-250	220-260	–	200-206	–	195-200	–	160-180
Potassium (K)	8-9.6	10-11.2	10-15	10-11.2	8.2-14.4	–	6.8	–	5.8-7.4	–	3.8-6.4

All values of physico-chemical parameters except pH and temperature are expressed in mg/L

Table 4. Baseline Data for Wetland Hydrology

Wetland	Inflow (m3/ days)	Area (hectare)	Water depth (m)	Volume (m3 x 104)	Hydraulic Detention (days)
Crocodile Jheel	10473	16	0.95	15.2	14.5
Taltala Jheel	23838	14	0.52	7.28	3.0
Khudi-I Jheel	23839	8	0.50	4.0	1.7
Khudi-II Jheel	23839	4.5	0.86	3.87	1.6
Loha Jheel	23839	5.0	0.81	4.05	1.7

Table 6. Biological Indicators : Phytoplankton

Taxa	Ponds					
	Croco-dile	Taltala	Khudi -I	Khudi -II	Khudi -III	Loha
CYANOPHYCEAE						
Microcysits sp.	+	+	+	+	+	+
Oscillatoria sp.	+	+	+	+	+	+
Anabeana sp.	+	+	+	+	+	+
Nostoc sp.	+	+	–	+	–	+
Spirulina sp.	+	+	+	–	–	–
CHLOROPHYCEAE						
Chalmydomonas sp.	+	+	+	+	+	+
Volvox sp.	+	+	+	+	+	+
Pediastrum sp.	+	+	–	+	+	–
Tetraspora sp.	+	+	+	+	+	–
Spirogyra sp.	+	+	+	+	+	–
Ulothrix sp.	+	–	–	+	+	+
Cladophora sp.	+	–	+	+	+	–
Oedogonium sp.	+	+	+	+	+	+
BACILLARIOPHYCEAE						
Cymbella sp.	–	–	+	+	+	+
Navicula sp.	–	+	+	–	–	+
Cyclotella sp.	+	+	+	–	–	+

\+ = Present
– = Absent

Table 7. Biological Indicators : Zooplankton

Taxa	Ponds					
	Croco-dile	Taltala	Khudi -I	Khudi -II	Khudi -III	Loha
PROTOZOA						
Amoeba proteus	+	+	+	+	+	+
Paramoecium sp.	+	–	–	–	–	–
Dinomonus sp.	+	+	+	+	+	–
ROTIFERA						
Filinia sp.	+	+	+	+	+	+
Keratella sp.	+	+	+	+	+	+
Brachionus sp.	+	+	+	+	+	+
Polyasthra sp.	–	+	–	–	–	–
CLADOCERA						
Daphnia sp.	+	+	+	+	+	–
Leptodora sp.	+	+	–	+	+	+
COPEPODA						
Cyclops sp.	+	+	–	+	+	–
Diaptomus sp.	+	+	+	+	+	+
Nauplii (Larvae)	+	+	+	+	+	–
DIPTERA						
Chironomus sp.	+	+	+	+	–	–
NEMATODA						
Planeria sp.	+	+	+	+	+	+

+ = Present – = Absent

Table 11. Fish Production

Sr. No.	Wetland	Water Area (Hectares)	Total Fish (Tonnes)	Annual Productivity Per Hectares (Tonnes)
1	Crocodile Jheel	16	39.50	2.47
2	Taltala Jheel	14	69.00	4.93
3	Khudi-I Jheel	8	56.00	7.00
4	Khudi-II Jheel	11	40.00	3.64
5	Loha Jheel	5	39.00	7.80
	Total		243.50	25.84

Table 8. Biological Indicators : Phytoplankton Population (March, 1990)

Sampling points	Total Phytoplankton counts (Org/m^3)	Percent Organisms in Group						No. of species present	Shannon Weaver's Diversity Index
		Cyanophyceae	Chlorophyceae	Euglenophyceae	Xanthophyceae	Bacillariophyceae	Chrysophyceae		
Crocodile	77500.00 + 1204.42	38.96+3.10	36.36+2.88	3.89+0.97	5.19+1.09	–	15.58	7	1.40
Taltala	47000.00 + 1688.66	32.76+1.72	56.90+3.51	–	6.90+1.76	3.45+0.93	2.68	7	1.33
Khudi-I	20500.00 + 1018.52	56.55+2.70	12.87+0.95	12.20+1.80	8.57+1.88	9.81+0.16	–	6	1.42
Khudi-II	22000.00 + 1118.21	54.55+2.10	13.64+0.98	9.09+2.31	–	22.73+2.10	–	4	1.67
Khudi-III	27000.00 + 1270.11	74.07+3.52	11.11+0.88	14.81+1.99	–	–	–	5	1.08
Loha	43000.00 + 2332.75	53.49+2.95	34.88+3.10	4.65+2.32	6.98+1.55	–	–	7	1.50

Table 9. Biological Indicators : Zooplankton population (March, 1990)

Sampling points	Total zoo-plankton counts (Org/m3)	Percent Organisms in Group					No. of species present	Shannon Weaver's Diversity Index
		Protozoa	Rotifera	Cladocera	Copepoda	Nematoda		
Crocodile	822.50 + 3.21	–	27.27 + 2.31	36.36 + 2.13	36.36 + 12.20	–	7	1.56
Taltala	1610.00 + 20.21	15.21 + 3.55	39.13 + 3.51	4.34 + 0.55	41.30 + 3.55	–	7	1.33
Khudi-I	850.50 + 2.56	12.00 + 2.98	28.00 + 2.12	16.00 + 1.68	44.00 + 3.07	–	5	1.82
Khudi-II	1015.00 + 130.22	–	13.79 + 1.55	17.24 + 1.22	68.96 + 2.88	–	4	1.20
Khudi-III	385.00 + 3.56	54.54 + 13.25	27.27 + 2.31	– + 2.11	18.18	–	3	1.41
Loha	560.00 + 38.20	81.25 + 12.05	·	18.75 + 1.78	–	–	3	0.70

Table 10. Bio-Magnification of Heavy Metals

	Pb	BCF	Magnification (%)	Zn	BCF	Magnification	Cu	BCF	Magnification (%)	Cr	BCF	Magnification (%)
Water	0.09	–	–	0.29	–	–	0.12	–	–	0.03	–	–
Phytoplankton	0.28	3.111	67.857	0.36	1.565	36.111	0.28	2.333	57.142	0.04	1.333	25
Zooplankton	0.30	3.333	70.000	0.41	1.783	43.90	0.32	2.667	62.5	0.05	1.667	40
Small fish	0.41	4.556	78.049	1.01	4.391	77.72	0.58	4.833	79.31	0.09	3.0	66.7
Large Fish	0.46	5.111	80-.435	1.03	4.478	77.67	0.61	5.083	80.33	0.11	3.667	72.7

All values are in ug/Kg of sample.
BCF = Bioconcentration Factor

Table 12. Performance Evaluation of Wetlands

Wetland	Influent BOD (mg/L)	Cumulative % of BOD Removal	Surface BOD loading Rate (Kg/hr/day)	Cumulative Fecal coliform removal efficiency (%)
Crocodile Jheel	140.0	85.7	91.6	26.67
Taltala Jheel	77.0*	–	131.1	99.4733
Khudi-I Jheel	27.2	64.68	83.4	99.9906
Khudi-II Jheel	23.2	69.87	69.3	99.9947
Loha Jheel	15.0	80.52	58.3	99.9980

*Flow composited average BOD of five outfall (KR-1, Univ-1, HP-1, Hide-1)

Baseline data collection revealed that :

* There was insignificant variation in the total wastewater flow
* Based on the species diversity indices, phyto and zoo plankton productivity wetlands can be classified as polluted to highly polluted
* Presence of heavy metals (Pb, Cu, Zn and Cr) in the industrial wastewater results in biomagnification factor of 3.7 to 5.1
* Low dissolved oxygen in the pond water during pre-monsoon period resulted into significant fish kill
* Wetlands were highly effective in removal of organic matter (overall BOD removal 80 %) and pathogen removal (overall removal 99 %)

5. IMPACT PREDICTION

Impact of nutrients on phyto and zoo plankton productivity was estimated using ecosytem dynamics model developed by NEERI.

6. IMPACT EVALUATION

In the present case wastewater was being discharged in the wetlands. Hence, it was not possible to collect data for pristine environment. Impact of project was evaluated against non-polluted similar ecosystems. Based on this environmental management plan was devised.

7. ENVIRONMENTAL MANAGEMENT PLAN

The problems due to excessive nutrients, higher Biochemical Oxygen Demand (BOD), Chemical Oxygen Demand (COD), higher concentration of heavy metals and imbalance planktonic (phytoplankton and zooplankton) growth reduces ecosystem productivity. These problems could be overcome through improvement in the quality of water inflowing in the wetlands. This in turn warrants treatment of raw sewage before entering wetlands. Treatment options include physical, chemical and biological processes.

EMP preapred for minimizing adverse impacts on wetland ecosystem include :

* Waste stablization ponds for pretreatment of wastewater
* Use of macrophytes as toxicant absorber in jheels to reduce the heavy metal levels
* Mixed culture consisting *Tilapia mossambica* and Indian major carps i.e. *Catla catla, Labeo rohita, C. mrigala* and *Cyprinus carpio* to improve the jheel water quality
* Biogas generation using macrophytes as resource

After EMP implementation, primary (plankton production) and secondary productivity (fish production) will improve. The secondary productivity will be 17 to 20 tonnes/ha/yr. instead of existing 7 to 8 tonnes/ha/yr. So, additional income will meet the expenditure of the maintenance of the system.

Table 13. Impact Evaluation

Indicator	Impact on Wetland	
	Project Without EMP	Project with EMP
Hydrological		
Flowrate	SA	NI
Flowrate distribution	SA	NI
Water surface elevations	NI	NI
Marsh surface elevations	NI	NI
Flood-frequency and intensity	NI	NI
Physico-chemical		
pH	SA	NI
Temperature	SB	NI
DO	SA	SB
BOD	HA	SB
Suspended solids	HA	NI
Nitrogen	SA	SB

Phosphorus	NI	NI
Pesticides	SA	NI
Heavy metals	SA	NI
Biological/Ecological Autoecologial		
Density of species	SA	SB
Frequency of species	SA	SB
Indicator species	SA	SB
Population		
Regenerative capacity	SA	SB
Community		
Growth form and structure	SA	SB
Seral stage in succession	SA	SB
Diversity index	SA	SB
Importance value index	SA	SB
Limnology		
Ecological pyramid	SA	SB
Food Chain	SA	SB
Primary productivity	SA	SB
Biomagnification	SA	SB

Legend : HA : Highly adverse; SA : Slightly adverse; NI : No impact ; SB : Slightly beneficial; HB : Highly beneficial

Impact evaluation for project with and without EMP scenarios is presented in Table - 13 which demonstrates efficacy of EMP.

CASE STUDY -2

KEOLADEO NATIONAL PARK (BHARATPUR, INDIA) - AN ECOSYSTEM STUDY

P.A. Azeez and V.S. Vijayan

Salim Ali Centre for Ornithology and Natural History
Coimbatore, Tamil Nadu, India - 641 010

THE PARK

The Keoladeo National Park, one of the famous waterfowl reserves in the subcontinent, is situated between 27°7.6 to 27°12.2'N and 77°29.5' to 77°33.9'E and covers an area of 2900 hectares (map). The Park, separated from the surrounding agricultural fields by a masonry wall, is more or less flat with a gentle slope towards the center. The submersible area, is approximately 850 hectares. Several earthern dykes and sluice gates constructed to facilitate water management divide the wetland into many unequal compartments.

Origin of the Park

The park, formerly known as keoladeo Ghana, has its origin from a natural depression. This depression, an evanescent wetland, at the confluence of rivers Gambhir and Banganga, was developed into a waterfowl reserve by water management about two and a half century back by the then ruler of Bharatpur. An earthern dyke known as Ajanbund, approximately one kilometer south-west of the park was constructed sometime in mid-18th century by Suraj Mahl, the then ruler of the princely state of Bharatpur (Vijayan, 1994) to protect the town from flood and also to raise crops after draining off the water. These types of earthen dykes and canals were an integral part of the traditional water management in the region. The main objectives of the rulers in converting the area into a permanent wetland and waterfowl reserve were to develop the area for (a) game hunting, (b) as a refuge for the unwanted cows from surrounding villages, and (c) providing grazing ground for buffaloes and village cattle. Since late 19th century a series of development activities have been undertaken in Keoladeo Ghana. A fence was raised around approximately 26 sq. km area and *Acacia nilotica* planted along the dykes and mounts in the early decades of the present century. Prior to this, no heronries existed in the wetland (Vijayan, 1994). The Keoladeo Ghana was declared a bird sanctuary in 1956, a National Park in 1980 and a Ramsar site in 1982. Since 1985 the area is included in World Heritage Sites.

Climate

The climate of Bharatpur is sub-humid to semi-arid and is characterized by hot dry weather, dust storms, low humidity and scanty drizzles. Although rain sets in by late June, the major portion of the rain is received during July to September. The post monsoon period is marked by rapid fall of temperature and occasional showers. The winter is cold and chilly. In winter Bharatpur also receives occasional showers due to northwestern disturbances.

Biological Cycle in the Park

The biological cycle of the Park starts with the monsoon, which sets in Bharatpur towards the end of June or the beginning of July. With the advent of monsoon the seeds germinate; rhizomes and tubers sprout. Water released from Ajanbund, through Ghana canal, bring into the Park millions of fry. A number of air-breathing fishes breeds in the deeper portions of the wetland. With monsoon (or towards the end of June) herony species, especially Openbill stork, start making nests and wait for water to come in. With the release of water the park becomes very active with thousands of colonial breeding birds busy making nests. Most of these birds complete nesting and bring out the chicks in October. Openbill storks feed the young mainly with molluscs which are abundant during the early inundation stage. Painted Stork which requires larger fingerlings delay laying so that the hatching synchronize with the availability of prey in preferred size. With the onset of monsoon resident ducks also commence nesting. Migratory waterfowl arrive in mid-September and their population reaches a peak during December January. From February the

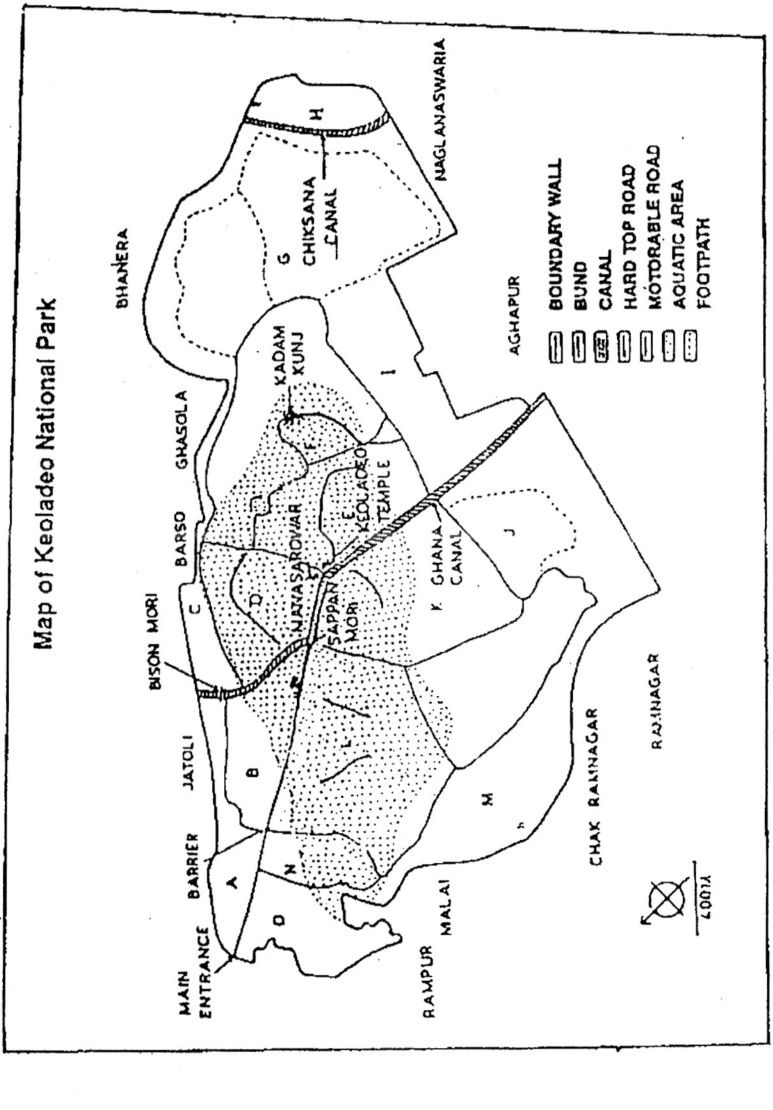

Map of Keoladeo National Park

waterfowl start return migration and by mid-March most of them would have left the Park. Water recedes gradually and towards May-June it is limited only to a few pools. A large number of fish congregated in these pools only to get devoured by birds and terrestrial carnivores, or to die and recycle back into the nutrient pool of the ecosystem.

Salient Features of the Study

The Bombay Natural History Society undertook an integrated, multi-disciplinary study on the Keoladeo National Park Ecosystem in 1980 under the leadership of late Dr. Salim Ali sponsored jointly by the US Fish & Wildlife service and the Ministry of Environment and Forests, Government of India. The study created a massive amount of data on various aspects of the system. Presently an attempt is made to model the Park ecosystem at SACON.

The major objectives of the study were to (a) analyze the ecology of the park, (b) identify the critical factors affecting the system, and (c) develop suitable management options for the park from a conservation perspective.

The important components of the ecosystem which were studied are listed in Table 1. Attempts have been made to trace the various trophic relations of the biotic components. Recognizing the role of people living in the surrounding areas of the Parks, the study was extended to examine the socio-economic aspects also.

Table 1. Various components of the Keoladeo National Park Ecosystem Study

Ecosystem Components		Salient features
Abiotic		
1	Temperature	Bharatpur faces extremes of temperature ranging from a minimum of 0-2°C (winter) to maximum of 48-50°C (in summer). Annual average maximum temperature was 30.8 to 35.1°C and minimum 16.9 to 22°C (Vijayan 1991).
2	Humidity	Average 62.5 ± 10.5% (Vijayan 1991)
3	Rainfall	Largely the rain was from southwest monsoon. Average rainfall for the last 100 years was 655 mm and for the last 10 years 496 mm (Vijayan, 1991).

4	Evapo-transpiration	Evapo-transpiration was in the range of 167 to 238 cm (Vijayan 1991).
5	Infiltration and baseflows	Infiltration was comparatively low except in certain points in different blocks of the wetland. The average infiltration in aquatic blocks was 44 mm/month. The soil is basically alluvial clay. Less clayey lenses are present in the wetland, which may function as ground water recharge sites (Vijayan 1991, *Azeez et al*, 1991).
6	Water table	Varied considerably in the park as well as in the surrounding villages (Azeez *et al.*, 1992).
7	Soil	Thick alluvium, saline soils are present in certain pockets (Vijayan, 1991).
8	Surface water quality	Of the twelve important water quality parameters examined, pH, DO, EC, alkalinity and dissolved CO_2 showed notable variation during the post 1982 period. The water which was slightly acidic in pre-1982 period turned alkaline later. DO was high in pre 1982 period (Vijayan 1991).
9	Ground water quality	Hardness, alkalinity, chloride, EC and sulfate was high in ground water, in contrast with the surface water of the wetland. Hardness varied from 102 to 2104 mg/1 as $CaCO_3$. The ground water inside the Park was slightly low in hardness than water in the village (Vijayan 1991).
10	Water budget (referred later in the text under management)	Different components (various inflows and outflows), of the water budget for the Park were estimated. Main among them which decide the hydroperiod are the inflow of water from Ajanbund, and evapo-transpiration. Surface inflow due to rain is comparatively low (Vijayan 1991).
11	Phytoplankton	The main phytoplankton groups were chlorophytes, desmids and myxophytes. Towards the later half of 1980s myxophytes were dominant. During 1982 to 1984 the plankton density showed a discernible increase. But it started decreasing since then reaching the lowest density in 1986. In 1987, although it was a drought year, the plankton density showed an increase. Plankton density was inversely related to macrophyte density. (Vijayan 1991)
12	Zooplankton	Cladocerans, copepodes, ostracodes and rotifers were the major zooplankton. The seasonal and annual variation of the zooplankton followed more or less the same pattern of phytoplankton (Vijayan 1991).

13	Planktonic primary productivity	The gross planktonic primary productivity in surface and bottom waters was low from 1983 to mid 1986. Since then until 1989 the productivity was higher. The mean productivity value for surface water for the period 1983-1986 was 0.138 gC/m^3/h and for 1986 to 1989 it was 247 gC/m^3/h. In bottom water the productivity was lower than that of the surface. High macrophyte biomass reduces planktonic primary productivity (Vijayan 1991).
14	Aquatic Macrophytes	In all 96 species of wetland plants coming under 66 genera and 36 families were recorded. The species with highest biomass during post 1982 period was *Paspalum distichum*, an amphibious grass. The macrophyte biomass kept on increasing since 1983 till the drought in 1986 and 1987. Even after the drought the biomass was quite high. Various methods for macrophyte control were tested *in situ*. But none were found effective (Prasad 1986, Davis *et al.*, 1988, George 1988, Vijayan *et al.*, 1990, Vijayan 1991).
15	Macrophyte decomposition	Decomposition of select species of major macrophytes were studied. The decomposition rate differed among species. The decay of plant matter led to considerable change in water quality (Davis *et al.*, 1988, Nadarajan and Azeez 1991, Vijayan 1991).
16	Terrestrial plants	281 species of angiosperms were recorded. Vegetation maps showing eleven major physiognomic types and detailed distribution of various plant communities were prepared. Productivity, biomass and phenology of grasses, sedges, herbs, shrubs and trees were studied. Various methods for control of the terrestrial grass were also tested *in situ*. (Perennou 1987, Perennou and Ramesh 1987, Prasad 1989, Haque 1990, Vijayan 1991).
17	Column water macro-invertebrates and insects	The column water macro-invertebrates includes insects, molluscs and oligocheates. The insect orders present were ephemeroptera, odonata, hemiptera, lepidoptera, trichoptera, neuroptera, plecoptera and diptera. The biomass, number and species composition were related with dissolved oxygen. Insect groups which can tolerate low oxygen level got dominant (Vijayan 1991).
18	Benthic invertebrates	Molluscs were the dominant benthic fauna. Oligocheates were also present. There was notable decrease in molluscs since 1984 (Vijayan 1991).

Vertebrates		+
19	Fish	43 species of fish belonging to 8 orders, 16 families and 31 genera were recorded. Only six species of fish breed in the Park. The rest are recruited from Ajanbund. Major source of fry are the breeding sites, the perennial ponds, in the river Gambhir. Habitat utilization of various species were studied and was found that most non-airbreathing fish prefer open water and open water with submerged vegetation habitats. Species richness and diversity were minimum in *Paspalum* dominated area. The food habits of 10 major species were also studied (Kumar 1990, 1992, Kumar and Vijayan 1988).
20	Amphibians	Seven species of amphibians belonging to three families (bufonidae, microhylidae and ranidae) were present in the park (Vijayan 1987).
21	Reptiles	Seven species of turtles were present in the Park. Ecology of select species of turtles such as Indian flap shell were studied. Eight species of lizards and thirteen species of snakes were recorded. The Park has 43 python burrows and more than 100 pythons. Ecology of python was also studied (Bhupathy 1990, Bhupathy and Vijayan 1989a, b, 1993, 1995).
22	Waterbirds	The habitat requirements, food and feeding habits and comparative abundance of migratory waterfowl, resident ducks, piscivorous birds, Jacanas, raptors, moorhens, Siberian crane and Sarus crane were studied. The abundance of waterfowl had significant positive correlation with water input. The change in habitat has altered the composition of waterfowl. Between 1983-84 and 1985-86 the grass preferring species increased by 40% (Bhupathy 1985, 1991, Prakash 1990, Ramachandran 1993, Ramachandran and Vijayan 1994, 1995, Sridharan 1989, Sivasubramanian 1991, Vijayan and Vijayan 1987).
23	Terrestrial birds	Landbird community, habitat preference and breeding seasonally of the terrestrial birds were studied. 23% of the birds were recorded in the mixed vegetation, while 17% each in Kadam groves and savanna woodland and 22% in grass savanna. The study also examined the role of plant phenology on landbird community and breeding seasonality (Sundarmoorthy 1991).

24	Mammals	Six species of large herbivores and six of small carnivores occur inside the Park. The study on mammals included population, biomass, habitat utilization and food preference. Except the feral cattle no other mammalian species had an increase in population. Wild Boar showed a sudden increase in number during 1985-86 and remained more or less the same all through the later years (Haque 1990).
25	Environmental contamination	The Park gets water from outside which may bring in a number of pollutants such as heavy metals and pesticides. Heavy metals contamination in the water bodies, fish and birds outside and inside the park were examined. Pesticide contamination were also studied in water, birds and eggs (Muralidharan *et al.*, 1992, Muralidharan 1993, 1995, Vijayan 1987).
26	Socio economics of the village around the Park.	Based on the closeness to the park 10 out of 18 villages were selected for the study. The economy of the villages were mostly agriculture based. Prior to 1982 they were depending more on buffaloes for income and fuel. After the ban on grazing the number of livestock in villages how decreased and the villagers have opted for other occupations (Azeez 1992, Azeez *et al.*, 1992).
27	Tourism	A study was undertaken to find out the type of visitors to the park, the problems faced by tourists and also to find means for encouraging tourism (Vijayan 1991).

Major Management Issues

The most important issues concerning the sustainable management of Keoladeo National Park : (a) water management, (b) quality of water, (c) fish supply to Park, (d) management of aquatic grasses and sedges, and (e) management of the populations of wild ungulates and feral cattle.

Water management is the single most important factor determining the ecological characteristics of the park. Water is let into the park every monsoon from Ajanbund through Ghana canal. The quantum of water available varies according to the vagaries of monsoon. The lowest quantity of water received was 0.017 million m^3 in 1986 and the highest 15.32 million m^3 in 1985. The inadequate supply of water affects the whole ecosystem. Of late the paucity of water has become a serious threat to the existence of the wetland.

Of the two rivers traditionally supplying water to the Ajanbund, the Banganga has become ineffective since many years because of growing human demands. The Gambhir, the other river also does not have sufficient water. Failure in timely supply of sufficient water leads to drop in fish availability, failure of heronries, fall in migratory waterfowl, mortality of turtle, low primary productivity and invasion of the wetland by terrestrial species such as *Vetiveria zizanioides, Acacia nilotica* and *Prosopis juliflora*.

Time of flooding, maintenance of water level, and duration of dry period are the three vital aspects in water management of Keoladeo National Park. The annual cycle of many plant and animal species commences with the release of water. Water level, rapidity of supply and the time of flooding determines to a great extent the formation of macrophyte community and the availability of different micro habitats such as open water and low grass areas, which are the preferred feeding habitats for many waterfowl. The dry spell is important because it enhances the decomposition of organic matter and release of nutrients. The flooding of the whole wetland in summer, hence, may cause a net accumulation of undecomposed organic matter and speeding up of eutrophication.

Water from Ajanbund may contain a number of pesticides. The surrounding area of the park has agriculture, where agrochemiscals are used in large quantities. Many bird eggs from the Park are contaminated with pesticides. The water remains stagnant in the Park for long period, giving ample scope for organochlorines and other contaminants with long half-life to get concentrated. Hence, the quality of water supplied to the Park have to be regularly monitored.

Breeding cycle of almost all the heronry species is synchronized with the influx of fry and their growth in the wetland. Recruitment of fish within the wetland is low in contrast with that from Ajanbund. Fry of about 37 species of fish are found in the incoming water. Major species among them are *Cirrhinus* sp., *Oxygaster* sp., and *Chanda* sp. Number of fry which entered the park during 1983-89 varied from 3.3 to 65 million. Major source of these fry are the ponds and reservoirs on the course of the river Gambhir. To guarantee the supply of fry, the breeding sites of fish outside the Park have to be preserved and fishing in these areas during the initial stages of monsoon needs to be controlled.

Most of the fish drawn from Ajanbund get exhausted by March - April when only resident species, mostly air-breather, are available. Only six species of fish namely *Channa punctatus, C. striatus, C. marulius, Heteropneustes fossilis, Claris batrachus and Colissa fasciata* breed inside the park. These fish breed in deeper areas of the wetland, mainly in the Manasarover and the pond by the side of Seetharam temple. These breeding sites inside the Park have to be maintained.

The wetland ecosystem is highly productive and hence, absence or removal of a major primary consumer leads into net accumulation of organic matter. In the case of Keoladeo National Park the Major consumer since its origin was buffaloes. Removal of the primary consumer and high input of nutrients through water supply and also from guano from thousands of resident and migratory birds have led to chocking up to the wetland with macrophytes. Drastic changes in the macrophyte community and wetland habitat have also occurred. The habitat heterogeneity, essential to support a variety of waterfowl and heronry species, was drastically reduced. Control of the macrophytes have become vital for the long term sustenance of the wetland system.

The population of wild mammals is a matter of concern in the Park. The population of blackbuck and chital has declined the last few decades. Wild boar was the only wild mammals which had shown any increase in population. The heavy competition with domestic cattle prior to 1983 when there were about 6000 buffaloes, must have kept the population at lower level. And the population increased later when the competition was almost absent. In 1989 there were more than 1000 feral cattle in the park. The feral cattle hardly feed in wetland area and have no impact on the aquatic macrophytes.

Impact of the Post-1982 Management Strategy on the Wetland System

The change in status of Keoladeo Ghana from a sanctuary to a National Park was followed by a change in the management strategy for the area. In 1982, buffalo grazing and harvesting of grass in the Park by villagers were banned. The present study proves that it was the single most important reason for the deterioration of the habitat. Since centuries buffaloes were grazing in the area where grass was growing profusely. The net annual productivity of aquatic macrophyte in the Park varied between 3.7 to 3 5 MT/ha (Table 2). About 15 tons of grass are also removed by villagers. In 1983 the biomass of *Paspalum distichum* alone was only 5.5 MT/ha while in 1986 it had rose up to 26 MT/ha. Buffaloes were keeping these highly productive macrophytes under control for ages. A single buffalo consumes approximately 12 kilogram dry weight of grass per day. The removal of buffaloes, an integral component of the system for centuaries, lead literally to clog the Park with macrophyte biomass. Buffaloes and geese prefer *Paspalum distichum* and feed selectively on it. Moreover buffaloes while grazing trample large quantity of macrophytes. During the post 1982 period the *Paspalum distichum* has become excessively dense and caused : (a) considerable decrease in open water area, (b) reduction in the floating vegetation, (c) change in water quality, (d) change in species composition of the fish community, (e) wide fluctuation in waterfowl population and composition, (f) decrease in breeding population of heronry species, and (g) decrease in Siberian Crane habitats.

Table 2. Annual net macrophyte productivity in wetland (metric ton/ha)

Macrophyte category	1983	1984	1985	1986	1987	1988
Emergent	9.9	10.5	21.1	33.1	2.2	4.2
Submerged + floating	2.9	1.5	1.5	1.9	1.5	0.5
Total	12.8	12	22.6	35	3.7	4.7

Paspalum distichum grows very fast and invades the area of sparse vegetation in the water body, and forms a thick mat. This results in decrease of open water area, submerged and floating vegetation. The large quantity of biomass also settles down at the bottom and leads to reduction in depth. The invasion of Paspalum mats decimated plants such as *Nymphaea pubescence, Nymphaea nouchali, Nymphoides india* and *Nymphoides cristata*. The last two species have become very rare since 1984. Decomposition of the Paspalum mat causes reduction in the dissolved oxygen. The mat reduces light penetration and curtails photosynthetic oxygen production in water column. This may bring about a considerable anaerobic situation in bottom layers. It also causes change in the fish community. Only air breathers are equipped to tide over low oxygen level in water. Seven species of fish namely *Notopterus chitala, Labeo bata, L. fimbriatus, Chagunius chagunio, Lepidochephalus guntea, Eutropiichthys vacha* and *Channa gachua* have disappeared from the Park (Kumar and Vijayan 1988).

A number of waterfowl require habitats with a good proportion of open water and less grass habitats (Table 3). The few among those which need open water area are pochards, Coot, cormorants and Cotton Teal. Most ducks and Coot feed on submerged vegetation. Invasion of open water habitat by *Paspalum* has reduced the preferred habitat of the waterfowl. Areas packed with waterfowl during 1981-82 have become mostly barren. The decrease in open water has also affected breeding of heronries. Darter, cormorants, Painted stork and Ibis are the specially affected species. In certain areas, although the water was sufficiently deep, birds deserted the nests because no open water area was visible in the nesting sites. In 1985 when the grass was removed and open water area was made available the results were encouraging. Birds such as Painted Stork, egrets and herons feed in shallow water zones while cormorants and darter need deeper areas. The sight of open water and the teeming fingerlings may be one of the required stimulus for the birds for laying.

Table 3. Preferred habitat and water depth of select waterfowl species

Species	Most preferred habitat	Water depth (cm)
Pintail	Ipomoea-Grass, 30% grass, 21-100	
Common Teal	<30% grass, Open water	0-40
Gadwall	<30% grass-Ipomoea, Open water	0-60
Garganey Teal	<30% grass-open water	21-80
Wigeon	<30% grass, Ipomoea	0-40
Shoveler	<30% grass, Ipomoea, rooted floating vegetation	0-80
Coot	<30% grass, Ipomoea, open water	21-100
Greylag Goose	Grass-Ipomoea, <30% grass	21-60
Bar headed Goose	Grass, 50% grass	0-20

Ref : Vijayan 1991

The most effected species was the Siberian Crane. The crane feeds on rhizomes of *Scirpus tuberosus, Cyperus rotundus, Eleocharis dulcis*, and *Nymphaea* sp., and prefers 30-40 cm deep water zone. Hence, they restrict most of their activities to only certain areas in the park. Since 1983 *Paspalum* has invaded the Siberian Crane habitats affecting them in two major ways; (a) the *Paspalum* mat prevents the food species from sprouting and growing up leading to the decay of rhizomes, and (b) It was laborious for the bird to locate and extract the rhizomes underneath the thick mat. As a result the time required for one feeding about was five times (about 25 seconds, Vijayan and Vijayan 1989) more than what it was prior to the banning of buffaloes. According to Spitzer (1979) in 1975 only 6 seconds was required for one feeding bout. The longer time needed for feeding bout and also cuts the time available for other body maintenance activities such as preening, which are very important for migratory birds (Vijayan and Vijayan 1989). The usual proportion of time spent for feeding and no-feeding activities was 55:45. This has become 85:15 after the banning of buffaloes.

Cyperus alopecuroides, an amphibious perennial sedge, is another species which poses threat to the waterfowl habitat. This sedge grows in wet soil but has seen rapidly colonizing open water areas. Since 1984, in certain blocks of the Park such as E and D this species has colonized more than 75% of the open water area, the most preferred habitat for waterfowl. The slow flooding of wetland is conducive for this sedge to colonize shallow water zones. *Acacia nilotica* and *Prosopis juliflora* are two tree species which have invaded the shallow zones of the wetland, especially the habitats of Siberian Cranes. These species colonized the bulldozed area faster, if not flooded fast.

The khus grass, *Vetiveria zizanioides*, is another species which demands attention. Traditionally the species has been harvested by villagers for thatching as well as to extract the vetiver oil. WIth the declaration of the national park this practice also was stopped. Because of the unchecked growth, free from harvesting by villagers and also grazing cattle, the grass has become very dense in Koldahar area, a traditional blackbuck habitat. Blackbuck needs open short grassland. *Vetiveria* has also spread to adjacent blocks and encroached some of the habitats of Siberian Crane. *Desmostachya bipinnate* also has become abundant since 1982. *Desmostachya* in its sprouting and growing stage is grazed by livestock. Villagers harvest this grass and make ropes. Ban on harvesting and grazing and, a few accidental fires that occurred fostered the species to spread widely.

Various experiments were conducted to find an ecologically viable method for the control of macrophytes in the Park. A summary of these are given in Table 4. In case of *Paspalum* nothing was found effective (Vijayan *et al.*, 1990). However, from the observations on the pre-1982 ecology and the understanding developed from the study here and elsewhere, it is very logical to advocate an experiment with buffalo in the wetland.

Major Outcome of the Study

The study demonstrates the importance of a major primary consumer for long-term sustenance of a wetland and also the ecological impact of being totally indifferent towards the traditional uses of a system before developing and implementing a new management strategy.

A comprehensive management plan was developed from the decade long ecosystem study of the park. The recommendations were made with the tacit understanding that (a) the Park is not a self supporting system and waterfowl use water bodies in the surroundings extensively, (b) the Park is only a green island surrounded by villages and hence, their co-operation is critical for the preservation of the park, (c) People had been depending on the Park for fuel wood and fodder centuaries, and (d) water scarcity is a serious problem in the surrounding areas.

Table 4. Experiments to control the macrophytes

Problem grass	Experiments	Observations
Paspalum distichum	Clipping the above ground vegetation	Clipping enhances growth. After three months biomass double of that of the unclipped areas. Clipping induces auxins, the plant growth hormones. However, clipping underwater is effective in checking the growth (Middleton 1990).
	Clearing the vegetation with surface soil	Initial stages grass were sparse. After six months the grass biomass was similar to control sites
	Bulldozing	Not effective for : (a) the area is recolonized within two years, (b) disturbs the system by destroying the dormant plants, rhizomes, tubers, animals especially aestivating fish and reptiles and increases eutrophication, (c) is expensive and (d) areas bulldozed if not flooded immediately is colonized by *Acacia* and *Prosopis*.
	Burning	*Paspalum* is replaced by *Pseudoraphis spinescens*, a coarse grass less preferred by birds. In the second year the *Paspalum* reemerges.
	Drying	Paspalum gets considerably reduced by drying the area for long period. *Paspalum* can not vegetatively propagate in dry soil. However, after the next rains this species is replaced by *Pseudoraphis*, a grass not as palatable as paspalum
	Harvesting	Harvesting in drought years is effective. Harvesting when the area is moist encourages growth. Large numbers of villagers harvesting the grass may disturb the nesting birds and in impractical.

	Uprooting	Effective, but needs huge manpower. Deploying large number of people disturb the birds.
	Water level manipulation	Fast flooding during sprouting stage is effective. But this destroys plants such as *Nymphoides* (Mason and Van der Valk 1990).
	Buffalo grazing	Past experience shows this was effective. Domestic cattle are used in many western countries for controlling macrophytes.
Cyperus alopecuroides	Uprooting	Uprooting before fruiting is an effective method.
Vetiveria zizanioides	Harvesting by villagers (Manual removal)	Manual removal is effective. Hence villagers may be allowed to harvest under supervision.
	Controlled fire	Fire is also effective, but leads to enhanced growth of *Desmostachya bipinnata*.
Desmostachya bipinnata	Harvesting	Harvesting under supervision is a suitable method.

References : Vijayan *et al.*, 1990, Vijayan 1991).

REFERENCES

Azeez, P.A. 1992. Conservation conflicts : a case study of Keoladeo National Park, Bharatpur, Rajasthan, Greenage 1: 35- 45.

Azeez, P.A., N.R. Nadarajan and D.D. Mittal 1991. The impact of monsoonal wetland on ground water chemistry. Intern. Confer. Land-water interactions, New Delhi, 1991.

Azeez P.A., N.K. Ramachandran and V.S. Vijayan 1992. The socio-economics of the villages around Keoladeo National Park, Bharatpur, Rajasthan, India. Intern. J. Ecol. Environ. Sci. 18 : 1-15.

Bhupathy, S. and V.S. Vijayan 1995. Aestivation of turtles in Keoladeo National Park with special reference to *Lissèmys punctata*. J. Bombay Nat. Hist. Soc. (in press).

Bhupathy, S. and V.S. Vijayan 1991. Freshwater turtle fauna of eastern Rajasthan. J. Bombay Nat. Hist. Soc. 88 : 118-122.

Bhupathy, S. and V.S. Vijayan 1989. Status, distribution and general ecology of the Indian Python (*Python molurus molurus* Linn.) in Keoladeo National Park, Bharatpur, Rajasthan. J. Bombay Nat. Hist. Soc. 86 : 381-387.

Bhupathy, S. 1990. Blotch structure in individual identification of the Indian Python (*Python molurus molurus*) and its possible usage in population estimation. J. Bombay Nat. Hist. Soc. 87 : 399-404.

Bhupathy, S. 1985. Ecology of Purple Moorhen *Porphyrio porphyrio poliocephalus* (From January to April 1985) in Keoladeo National Park, Bharatpur M.Sc. Dissertation, Bharathidhasan University, Tiruchirapalli.

Bhupathy S. and V.S. Vijayan 1989. Predation on the Indian Flap- shell Turtle (*Lissemys punctata*) in Keoladeo National Park, Bharatpur, Rajasthan. Proc. Nat. Symp. Anim. Behav. In : B.H. Patel (ed), Behaviour, Sir P.P. Institute of Science, Bhavnagar, pp. 27-33.

Bhupathy, S. and V.S. Vijayan 1993. Aspects of the feeding ecology of *Lissemys punctata* (*Testudines : Trionychidae*) in Keoladeo National Park, Bharatpur. Hamadryad 18 : 13-16.

Bhupathy, S. 1991. Population and resource utilization of waterfowl in Keoladeo National Park, Bharatpur, Rajasthan. Ph.D. Thesis. Rajasthan University, Jaipur.

Davis, C.B., A.G. Van der Valk, D.H. Mason, B. Middleton and R. Williams 1988. Ecology of a semitropical monsoonal wetland in India-the Keoladeo Ghana National Park, Bharatpur, Rajasthan, p. 104.

George, J.M. 1988. Bio-ecology and population dynamics of the beetle *Crassida circumdata* Herbst in Keoladeo National Park, Bharatpur. Ph.D. Thesis, University of Agra.

Haque, M.N. 1990. Study of the ecology of wild ungulates of Keoladeo National Park, Bharatpur, Rajasthan. Ph.D. Thesis, Aligarh Muslim University.

Kumar C.R.A. 1990. The fish community of Keoladeo National Park, Bharatpur, Rajasthan, India. In : Hirano. R. and I. Hanyu (ed) Proc. II Asian Fisheries forum, Tokyo, Japan, pp. 385-388.

Kumar C.R.A. 1992. Community and habitat segrgation of fish in keoladeo national park, Bharatpur, Ph.D. Thesis, Kanpur University.

Kumar C.R.A. and V.S. Vijayan 1988. On the fish fauna of Keoladeo National Park, Bharatpur, Rajasthan. J. Bombay. Nat. Hist. Soc. 85 : 44-49.

Mason, D.H. and A.G. Van der Valk 1990. Life history characteristics of two floating leaf aquatic plants *Nymphoides indica* ktze and *N. cristatus* Roxb. ktze in a semitropical monsoonal wetland in India. Semi. Wetland Ecology and Management, Keoladeo National Park, Bharatpur, Bombay Natural History Society.

Middleton B. 1990. Effect of water depth and clipping frequency in the growth and survival of four wetland plant species. Aquat. Bot. 37 : 189-196.

Muralidharan S. 1993. Aldrin poisoning of Sarus cranes (*Grus antigone*) and a few granivorous birds in Keoladeo National Park, Bharatpur, India. Ecotoxicology 2 : 196-202.

Muralidharan S. 1995. Heavy metal contamination in and around the aquatic environs of Keoladeo National Park, Bharatpur. Ph.D. Thesis. Rajasthan University, Jaipur.

Muralidharan, S., A. Ragupathy and T. Sundaramoorthy 1992. Organochlorine residues in the eggs of selected colonial water birds breeding in Keoladeo National Park, Bharatpur, India. In : Roberts, R.D. and Bothwell M.L. (ed) Aquatic ecosystems in semi- arid regions for resources management. Symposium series 7. pp. 189-195, Environment Canada.

Nadarajan, N.R. and P.A. Azeez 1991. Changes in the nutrient content of macrophytes during decomposition. Intern. Confer. on Land-water interactions, New Delhi, 1991.

Perennou C. 1987. Vegetation map of Keoladeo National Park. French Institute of Pondicherry and Bombay Natural History Society, Bombay.

Perennous C and B.R. Ramesh 1987. Explanatory notes on the vegetation map of Keoladeo National Park. French Institute of Pondicherry and Bombay Natural History Society, Bombay.

Prakash , V. 1988. Status and ecology of raptors at Keoladeo National Park, Bharatpur, Rajasthan. Ph.D. Thesis, Bombay University.

Prasad, V.P. 1986. Wetland angiosperms of Keoladeo National Park, Bharatpur. J. Econ. Taxon. Bot. 12 : 457-466.

Prasad, V.P. 1989. Flora of Keoladeo National Park, Bharatpur. J. Econ. Taxon. Bot. 13 : 729-750.

Ramachandran N.K. and V.S. Vijayan 1994. Distribution and general ecology of the Status Crane (*Grus antigone*) in Keoladeo National Park, Bharatpur, Rajasthan. J. Bombay. Nat. Hist. Soc. 91 : 211-223.

Ramachandran N.K. and V.S. Vijayan 1995. Breeding biology of the pheasant tailed and bronze winged jacanas in Keoladeo National Park, Bharatpur. J. Bombay. Nat. Hist. Soc. (In press)

Ramachandran N.K. 1993. Ecology of the pheasant tailed and bronze-winged jacanas in Keoladeo National Park, Bharatpur, Rajasthan. Ph.D. Thesis, Bombay University.

Sivasubramanian C. 1992. Ecological investigations on piscivorous birds in Bharatpur, Rajasthan. Ph.D. Thesis, Saurashtra University, Gujarat.

Spitze P.R. 1979. The Siberian Crane at Bharatpur. In : J.C. Lewis (ed) Proc. 1978 crane workshop. Colorado State Univ. pp. 249-254.

Sridharan U. 1989. Ecology of resident ducks of Keoladeo National Park, Bharatpur, Rajasthan. Ph.D. Thesis, Bombay University, Bombay.

Sundaramoorthy, T. 1991. Ecology of terrestrial birds in Keoladeo National Park, Bharatpur, Rajasthan. Ph.D. Thesis, Bombay University Bombay

Viajayan, V.S. 1987. The proposed galvalume plant of General Engineering

Works and Keoladeo National Park- an impact assessment, Bombay Natural Society, Bombay, p. 337.

Vijayan, L. and Vijayan V.S. 1987. Status, distribution and ecology of the Siberian Crane at Keoladeo National Park, Bharatpur, India. Intern. Crane Workshop. China, Intern. Crane. Foundation, Wisconsin.

Vijayan, L. 1994. Keoladeo National Park Ecology, World Wide fund for Nature India, New Delhi, pp 77.

Vijayan, L. and Vijayan V.S. 1989. Wintering population of the Siberian Crane *Grus leucogernus* and its behaviors in Keoladeo National Park, Bharatpur, India. Asian Crane Congress, Saurashtra University, Wisconsin.

Vijayan V.S. 1987. Vertebrate Fauna of keoladeo National Park Bharatpur. Contribution 1. Bombay Natural History Society, Bombay.

Vijayan L., V.P. Prasad and V.S. Vijayan 1990. Seasonal and annual variations of the biomass of aquatic macrophytes and the effect of various management techniques. Seminar, Wetland Ecology and management, Keoladeo National park, Bharatpur, Bombay Natural History Society.

Vijayan V.S. 1991. Keoladeo National Park Ecology study 1980- 1990, Final Report. Bombay Natural History Society, Bombay.

CASE STUDY - 3

ENVIRONMENTAL IMPACT ASSESSMENT OF SUNDARBANS - A CASE STUDY

Pranabes Sanyal

Government of West Bengal

1. STATUS

Sundarbans delta, the largest prograding delta on globe provides richest biodiversity among any other intertidal forest on one hand and popularly transmits a chill being the "Land of fear" on the other. Two great rivers, the Ganges and Bramhaputra meet the Bay of Bengal along India and Bangladesh forming an intertidal zone of nearly 26000 sq.km. Within this an area of nearly 8000 sq. km. of Mangrove forests, tidal creecks and rivers in India and Bangladesh contain between 500 and 600 Bengal Tigers the largest single population to survive anywhere in the world. The Indian Sundarbans region covering an area of 9630 sq. km. have a Reserve Forest declared over 4623 sq. km. area having no human settlements inside. There are 3 sanctuaries viz. the Sajnakhali Wildlife sanctuary, Lothian island sanctuary and halliday Island sanctuary. The entire core area of Sundarbans Tiger Reserve had been declared as Sundarbans National Park. Reclamation started during the eighteenth century. The northern boundary of Sundarbans region was demarcated by Dampier-Hodges line running more or less from kakdwip on west to Basirhat on east. At present the reclaimed area contains a population of 3.4 million (1991 census) people having nearly 45 p.c scheduled casts and scheduled tribes as against a state average of 25 p.c.

The result of continuous reclamation caused an immature agricultural land capable of yielding only a single crop. The creek waters became more and more saline owing to lack of fresh water flow which is the effect of the neotectonic movements that titled the

Bengal basin eastwards and Ganges flow started coursing through the river Padma into Bangladesh. The large stretch of mangrove forests dwindled down to more than 50 p.c. and the first conservation approach was initiated in December, 1973 by lunching of Project Tiger over 2585 sq. km. of forest area to save this 61 p.c of India's total mangrove reserve. In 1983 the core area was declared a National park and in 1989 the total intertidal zone of 9630 sq. km. was declared as Sundarbans Biosphere Reserve. Sundarbans have also been included in the World Heritage List to preserve it for the prosterity.

2. UNIQUE FEATURES

i. Sundarban is the largest mangrove reserve on globe having greatest mangal biodiversity. Among 64 Nos. of mangal associates 33 Nos. of plants are "Mangrove Exclusive" species which only can be matched by Mahananda mangals of Orissa the tiny 225 sq.km. reserve.

ii. Sundarbans being 61 p.c. of India's total mangrove reserve acts as nursery for a number of fish and shell fish which forms the base food chain for entire coastal fishery of Eastern India.

iii. Sundarban is the only Mangrove Tigerland on globe.

iv. The large chunk of Sundarban Mangrove protects the Metropolies of Calcutta suburbs from the frequent gales originating from bay of Bengal diverting it either Southwards to Midnapore coast or Northwards to Sandwip coast.

v. Sundarban is the abode of a good number of highly endangered flora and fauna eg. the rare stilt rooted climber the *Acanthvs volubilis,* the Estuarine crocodile, the Salvator lizard, the Fishing Cat, the almost extinct Batagur River Terrapin, the Globally endangered marine Turtles and Horse-shoes.

3. PROBLEMS

The refractory terrain of Sundarbans poses of problems which needs urgent and extra attention in order to maintain the existing mangrove resources in perpetuity.

i. The winter irrigation in reclaimed Sundarbans is a priority area to be dealt with. The creek waters are unfit for irrigation and the ground water table is saline at shallow depths. The linear water storage channels have limited capacity. The yield of paddy is low in the immature reclaimed land.

ii. The population pressure is increasing but people remain

unemployed for a good part of year in this single crop area, thus they have to eke out their living from fishing, honey collection and wood cutting during slack season even venturing into tigerland.

iii. Conservation of mangroves have been attracting the Tiger Prawn post larvae in huge numbers. The local villagers catch them to sell it at aquaculture ponds, Whole family while get a sort of employment, the residual waters containing other Ichthyo-plankters are thrown carelessly on mudflats. This had caused a large-scale depletion of lesser Mullets like Parse (*Liza parsea*) & Bhangan (*L. taede*) in particular.

iv. The existing infrastructural facilities are unable to cope up with the mechanised efforts of Wood poachers to large extent, within innumerable creeks of this vast wilderness.

v. Drinking water supply is an urgent problem in Sundarbans. The potable water table is 300 to 400 mtrs. deep. At places thin fresh water aquifers are tapped at shallow depths eg. in Jambudwip and Marichjhapi island.

vi. Protection against soil erosion at vulnerable banks of creeks and rivers by erecting suitable soil conservation measures is often a great necessity because of unstable nature of mudbanks.

vii. Poaching of Marine turtles at the estuarine mouth when they gather for mating is also a similar problem as Mahanadi estuary of Orissa. The poaching of Deers and Tigers also needs constant alertness to contain with.

viii. The man-animal conflict is an ageold Problem in Sundarbans. The honey collectors honey comb the forests during the months of April and May. The permit holders gather wood and fire wood from the tigerland, resulting in tiger human conflict. The Rock bees (*Apis dorsata*) responsible for huge honey production of Sundarbans can not be domesticated at advantageous location. This conflict is thus unavoidable till date and is the root cause of creation of man eating tigers.

ix. Tiger straying within fringe villages is another ageold problem of Sundarbans. Sundarbans Tigers being non-territorial in nature, often confuse the buffer strip of mangrove along fringe villages to be part of their habitat and they swim across the rivers from main forest block to find easy cattle prey. Thus such tigers became habituated cattle lifters.

4. E I A - SUNDARBANS

Potential Environmental elements :

A. Physico-Chemical

(i) Land

- Soil is 'Typic Haploquept, Clayey, Hyper thermic'
- Salinity 15 ppt. average, Sodic clay is often Pyrite rich.
- Gentle slope, intertidal zones are reclaimed by embankments, 5000 km^2 reclaimed land, 4264 sq.km.

Mangrove forest, 366 km^2 restoration zone.

- Saline blank formations on 'geomorphic highs'

(ii) Ground Water

- Water table near surface (3 m depth)
- Water quality is saline, with occasional fresh water aquifer at 100 m. depth else at 300 m. depth.
- Potable water through deep tubewell or rainwater impoundments.

- Irrigation is only through 3 m. deep linear channels for trapping rain water.
- On some sandy island fresh water lenses occur on saline interface.

(iii) Surface Waters

- Creek waters are saline (8.2 to 28 ppt.)
- Tidal amplitude up to 5.5 mr.
- No irrigation is possible
- DO is lower on west and becomes 6 mg./l east of Thakuran river.
- Water quality is unfit at Hooghly estuary with high Coliform count and ciliate protozoa.
- Calcutta metropolis discharge sewage 396.9 t/d in Creeks of Sunderbans and 22.9 t/d in Hooghly.
- 85% dissolved metal settles between Sagar and Haldia 15% goes to open sea; 40% suspended metal goes to open sea.

- Salt wedge extents up to Diamond Harbour During monsoon outer estuary is less saline than mid and inner estuary.
- Due to lack of upstream flow the monsoon freshets float on salt water at estuary mouth with unbroken interface.
- Accelarated geomorphic action by rushing surf water remains underterred by scanty upstream river flow.

(iv) Atmosphere

- Rainfall 1750 mm. av.
- Excellent ambient air quality
- Storm or high gale at least once a year.

B. Biological

(i) Flora

- 4264 sq. kms. of Mangrove forest. (61% of India's total mangrove).
- Enteromorpha and Rhodophytes e.g. Caloglossa are frequent algae found in the west.
- Out of 64 Nos. of Mangals, 33 are true mangrove.
- Rare mangrove climber *Acanthus volubillis* is found to occur. As such, all mangrove plants are considered endangered.
- Productivity is 7.6 tC/h/y with root (21-27%).

Aquatic productivity is 4.3 tC/h/y.

(ii) Fauna

- Tiger land with Fishing cat, Leopard Cat, Chital, Pigs, Rhesus monkey, King Cobra, Kraits.
- Aquatic fauna consists of Estuarine Crocodile, Salvator lizard, Otters, Dolphins, Porpoise, Marine Turtles, Estuarine terrapines, Freshwater turtles.
- Zooplanktons consist of postlarve of Tiger Prawn, Copepodes, Noctaluca
- Benthic Crabs have 48 species including edible *Schylla serrata*, Horse shoes, *Cliberaneous padavensis*.

- Mullet fishes, Sharks and edible Oyster e.g. Crassaustrea cuculata, Anadara granosa.
- Rare Bird Goliath heron, rare terrapin Batagur baska, Hawksbill, Olive Ridley and green Turtle.
- Bengal Tiger, Fishing Cat, Crocodile, Smooth Indian otter, Salvator lizzard, gangetic Dolphin Batagur terrapin are endangered.
- Migratory ducks e.g. Pintails, Tufted Pochard.
- 90% of regional aquatic species predictably are found in mangrove swamp during one or more periods of their life cycle.

C. Human

(i) Health and safety

- Man-eating is an age old problem. Av. 48 Nos/y casualty came down to 30/y.
- Tiger straying, Crocodile and Shark casualty are common.
- Single crop land, people are below poverty level.
- Population 3.4 milion (45% Backward class)
- Diarrhoea is a problem.

(ii) Socio - economic

- 4 Colleges and a number of Schools.
- No industry.
- Tourism generates employment with launch and mechanised boats, tourist guides.
- Fishing, Honey collection, Wood cutting are employments.
- Farm labours.

(iii) Aesthetic and Cultural

- Both Hindus and Muslims worship Banbibi the Tiger Godess.
- 45000 numbers are annual tourist flow.
- Post larval prawn catching is family occupation Balance Ichthyoplankans get lost.

ENVIRONMENTAL IMPACT

Activities	Primary	Secondary	Tertiary	Mitigation
Sewage outfall	– Decrease of DO – Bioaccumulation of metallic pollutants PCBs – Upstream siltation rendering rivers dead e.g. Piali Bidyadhari	– Upstream reduction of post larval prawn/ mullete. – Damage to consumers to bioaccumulated fish/. shell fish. – Increase in erosion + Increase productivity after dilution	– Fall in number of higher predators eg. Otters – Accelerate seaweed production + Generate employment by algal culture	Sewage treatment – Utilise in sewage fed fishery –Mangrove plantation – Marine alagl extraction
Dam/Diversion	– Reduction in fresh water flow – Increase salinity – Accelerated geomorphic activity of sea water – Loss of bio-diversity	– Productivity loss – reduction of turtle nesting (Aribada) + Winter irrigation (Part) + Decrease in P4 intake. – Reduction innutrient	– Reduction in Coastal catches + Boost to Local economy – Stunted Mangroves saline blanks	
Forest exploration	– Habitat loss – Man animal conflict – Nutrient increase + Economic benefit - erosion – Productivity loss	– Biodiversity loss + Generates employment + Mitigates local fuel small wood needs. + Source of honey & bees was – killing of Tiger, Crocodile – Eutrophication	– Cyclone damage if over exploited - Decrease in population of fish and shell fish	– Sustainable planned exploitation – Minimise Man-animal conflict generate alternate employment through ecodevelopment
Reclamation	– Mangrove destruction – Loss of aquatic productivity (4tc/C/L/Y) – Decrease in export to coastal system –Loss of wind barrier – Decrease in nutrient removal	Destruction of genepool - decrease in catch of fish/ shell fish – Increase in soil erosion – Threat to local economy – Threat to human and cattle safety due to tiger straying	– Threat to endangered species – Loss of productivity of coastal ecosystem of east India.	Minimise erosion by (i) raising Mangrove plantation (ii) using geojuta (iii) using porcupines – Regular extraction of edible and agar yielding algore will minimise effect of

	– water pollution from drainage of reclaimed bud – Tiger straying + Economic (Agrl.)	– Threat to greater Calcutta from cyclone damage – Increase in Eutrophication		Eutrophication – Tiger straying may be minimised by timber errection of portable electric fence.
Agriculture	Mangrove destruction – Deplection of past larval prawn due to over collection (540 m/y) – Pollution due to toxic drainage from ponds – Impeding natural drainage – Moffia culture – Replacement of existing paddy fields + Generates employment	– Loss of productivity of creeks – Decrease in export to coast- Destruction of balance Ichthyoplanklets after postlarval collection – Siltation of creeks due to drainage blockable – Damage to human consumers offers, Dolphins etc. due to bioaccumulation – Socio economic problem	Decrease in catch of coastal fishery – Decrease in catch of mullets and other organic due to seed mortality. – Increased coastal erosion due to loss of drainage.	– Drug use can be mitigated by maintaining proper hygene – balance ichthyoplanktes can be released back to creek – Plant Mangrove in aqua culture areas – Semi-intensive practice

CASE STUDY - 4

EIA OF BHITARKANIKA WILDLIFE SANCTUARY

Preeti Govil

World-Wide Fund for Nature, India

1. BACKGROUND

The EIA of a development project having repercussions on the environment is primarily the responsibility of the project proponent and the government authorities. With the growing concern towards sustainable development, the Courts are adopting an activist attitude by compelling the government to do the EIA of the projects. In the present case study the EIA of the development activities going on in the Bhitarkanika wildlife sanctuary was done by taking recourse to the legal action. In Bhitarkanika Sanctuary case, the Hon'ble Court has granted the stay order in a public interest litigation by Centre for Environmental Law, WWF India and directed the State to constitute EIA study committee. The terms of reference of the committee were :

- To study the impact of the fish landing centre at Talchua on the ecology of Bhitarkanika Sanctuary including the mass nesting of Olive Ridley sea turtles
- Whether boats plying from the fish landing centre will interfere with the nesting of sea turtles
- To study the impact of the improvement of the existing road, and construction of bridges on the ecology of the sanctuary
- Whether fish landing centres proposed at Tantiapal, Kharnasi and Jamboo attract Coastal Zone Regulations

- To suggest measures to mitigate the adverse impacts, if any, of the fish landing centres on Bhitarkanika ecosystem

It was pointed out by the committee that a assessment of the impacts of any anthropogenic activity like development projects on the environment involves evaluation of various primary and induced effects, both beneficial and adverse and suggestions for optimum total benefit to the activity as well as the environment. It has also accepted its serious limitation of time, resources and lack of expertise in preparing such type of report. The committee prepared the recommendation after receiving inputs from the government records, direct interaction with public, responses to public notice, visits to sites, published materials etc.

The major recommendation of the committee after the rapid EIA are:

- To take effective steps to curb influx of human population
- Ceiling on operation of mechanised boats
- Staffing and policing at vantage points
- Improvement of saline embankment and construction of bridges after taking mitigative measures like realignment of roads, strengthening the protection network with more check gates, additional staff and restriction on heavy commercial transportation
- Restoration of encroached land to Forest Department
- No aquaculture farms to be allowed within the sanctuary
- To undertake massive eco-development programme with goal as conservation of habitat with biotic diversity and sustainable use of natural resources with active involvement of local people
- All trawlers operating in area to have Turtle Extrusion Device
- Settlement of rights under Wildlife Protection Act 1972
- To undertake COMPREHENSIVE EIA pertaining to all developmental activities in the area for more detailed evaluation of the impacts of the highly eco sensitive area.

The EIA committee has emphasised the need of detailed and comprehensive EIA of the activities in this area as it is a fragile and unique ecosystem and wetland with a rich biodiversity.

Salient Features of the Site

Project Area:	Bhitarkanika Wildlife Sanctuary
Location:	The Bhitarkanika sanctuary is located in Orissa between latitude of 20" 4'North - 20" 8'North and latitude of 86". 45' East - 87" 50'East and covers an area of 672 sq. kms. in Bhadrakh and Kendrapara districts of Orissa. It lies in the river delta estuary of Brahmani, Baitarani and Kharasrota.
Legal status:	The Bhitarkanika Wildlife sanctuary was notified vide notification No. 6958/FFAH dated 22.04.1975 of the Government of Orissa. It is also a proposed National Park.
Physiognomy:	The Bhitarkanika Sanctuary is a unique mangrove system and is the second largest stretch of mangrove forests in the Indian mainland. The forests are coastal swamp forests, tidal swamp forest and mangrove forests. It is a transition or ecotone of sandy and muddy coast line. The soil varies from clayey loam to sandy loam.
Population: is approximately 1,20,000 in about 300 villages.	
Ecosystem and Biodiversity Value:	The area is coastal estuarine, mangrove ecosystem and wetland ecosystem. Floristically, the area is very rich and has 62 species out of the 67 known Indian Mangrove species e.g. Sundari (Heritiera), Sisumara (Xylocarpus), Bani (Avicennia), Guan (Exoecaria), Bandri (Bruguiera), Rai (Rhizophora). The fauna is also diverse and includes salt water crocodiles, monitor-lizards, Pacific Olive Ridley Sea Turtles, etc. The birds includes king fishers, storks, Herons, Egrets, white breasted water hens etc. The Gahirmatha beach in the sanctuary is the largest rookery of Olive Ridley Turtles in the world.

2. ISSUES

Various issues and constraints in the area are encroachment of forest land for paddy cultivation, rehabilitation, prawn culture, grazing, sporadic poaching, illicit fellings, uncontrolled fishing, construction of fishing jetties and other developmental activities without prior approval from the Forest Department is one of the major problems of the area.

In order to protect this unique ecosystem and to draw public attention towards its conservation, CEL, WWF- India initiated a PIL by filing a writ petition in the Hon'ble High Court of Orissa against the State of Orissa and Union of India on 22nd April, 1994. It is contended in the petition that the people, flora and fauna are directly and adversely affected by various development activities going on in and around the Bhitarkanika Sanctuary. The petitioner prayed for the following :

- to restrain state from constructing jetties, fishing complex, roads, ridges etc within and around the sanctuary
- to direct the State to provide peoper infrastucture personnel etc. for effective implementation of various legislations to protect and conserve the mangrove forest and the endangered species of wildlife of the Bhitarkanika Sanctuary and its surrounding areas
- to appoint a Committee to carry out an environmental impact analysis of the construction of the jetty, fishing complex, roads, bridges etc. and of the tiger prawn farming in brackish water and fishing by mechanised boats in and around the Bhitarkanika Wildlife Sanctuary and to determine the area which needs protection

The case is still pending in the court for the final hearing yet it is a precedent setting case in the field of wetlands EIA and the role which the NGOs and judiciary can play in protection and management of wetlands.

In this case the environment appraisal has been ordered by the court only when the issue was taken up by the NGO. The need of the hour is to create such an environmental awareness so that the project proponents, industrialists and the government on their own initiative start the EIA process as a part of the project cycle.

3. CONCLUSION

All the ecosystems have an important role to play but the productivity and multiple benefits of wetlands gives them a special significance. Therefore there should be a comprehensive EIA of any development project, programme or policies in or adjacent to Wetlands. For a successful long term strategy, socially equitable and ecologically sustainable development is a prerequisite. The EIA of development projects of Wetlands should thus adopt an integrated, holistic and multidiscipliary approach and the process should be integrated at the initial stages itself.